A Freelancer's Guide to Legal Entities

A Freelancer's Guide to Legal Entities

Alex D. Bennett, JD

BEP BUSINESS EXPERT PRESS

A Freelancer's Guide to Legal Entities
Copyright © Business Expert Press, LLC, 2018.

First published in 2018 by
Business Expert Press, LLC
222 East 46th Street, New York, NY 10017
www.businessexpertpress.com

ISBN-13: 978-1-94744-104-0 (paperback)
ISBN-13: 978-1-94744-105-7 (e-book)

Business Expert Press Business Law Collection

Collection ISSN: 2333-6722 (print)
Collection ISSN: 2333-6730 (electronic)

Cover and interior design by S4Carlisle Publishing Services
Chennai, India

First edition: 2018

10 9 8 7 6 5 4 3 2 1

Printed in the United States of America.

Abstract

Businesses are increasingly turning to freelancers to supply services that used to be provided by full-time employees or larger consulting firms. As a consequence, freelancing has become a dynamic, sophisticated, and potentially lucrative career choice. With these opportunities comes greater risk, as freelancers begin working in litigious industries and on projects with high dollar value. Many freelancers think about forming a limited liability entity, such as a corporation or limited liability company (LLC), as one way to manage their risk. But the decision about whether or not to form an entity, and what kind of entity is best, isn't necessarily easy, especially once the freelancer starts digging into the cloud of legal issues that surrounds organizing and managing a legal entity.

This book is a concise guide to business entities and related legal topics in the United States, designed specifically to help freelancers make informed decisions about how to structure and run their businesses. The goal is to provide freelancers with a framework for analyzing business risk before delving into the basic principles of sole proprietorships, LLCs, and corporations. We'll also explore important topics that every small business owner should understand: how limited liability works, legal issues related to business names, taxes, and contracts.

Keywords

business law, business naming, business organizations, contracts, corporation, corporate governance, freelancer, legal entities, liability, limited liability company, risk management, tax, trademark

Contents

Acknowledgments

I thank the generous contributions of time and thought by my readers and reviewers. Their advice helped make this book what it is. Thanks to my readers Austin Aslan, Linda Bennett, Adrienne Eaton, and Mark Krause for providing invaluable feedback. A special thanks to Steve Dolins, Jim Krause, and Arnie Lutzker for their professional insights. I would also thank my colleagues in the San Diego Professional Editors Network and the Editorial Freelancers Association for the valuable lessons they've taught me about freelancing. Above all, thanks to Sara for her support, ideas, and tireless rereadings.

Introduction

If you're reading this book, you have already started asking yourself important questions about how your freelance business should be organized. Maybe you're just getting started and still working on finding your first clients, building a reputation, and establishing a routine. Or perhaps you're a seasoned professional with a stable of clients and ample experience. Either way, you face the same questions: Should you conduct your business as an individual or would you be better off forming a legal entity, like a limited liability company (LLC) or corporation? What are the advantages and disadvantages of the different business forms? How would operating a legal entity affect your workload and finances?

One reason freelancers find these questions hard to answer is that freelancing itself has evolved. We all can agree that freelancers are a kind of independent contractor—that is, they work for clients without becoming their clients' employees. A few industries, like publishing, have used freelancers on large projects for decades. But many businesses and individuals are only just beginning to embrace the freelance market as a source for quality workers. Today, freelancers provide their business clients with a wide range of services that conventional employees used to provide. Individuals, too, are increasingly calling on freelancers to perform services that used to be only available from larger businesses. The pool of potential clients and projects has grown more diverse, offering great opportunities to make a good living.

With opportunity comes risk. Maybe you have litigious clients or work in a high stakes industry where an unsympathetic lawyer is lurking behind every project. Maybe your business involves uncomfortable financial obligations. Or maybe your freelancing income and expenses are raising tax headaches. Organizing a legal entity is one way to get ahead of these and other kinds of risk, and to protect your personal assets.

This book is a short course in the basics of business organizations in the United States, directed specifically to the needs of freelancers. **The goal is to give you a sound foundation in basic principles, so you can**

understand the options and issues you face when analyzing your own situation. Deciding how to organize your business involves not only knowing the kinds of advantages a legal entity provides but also the obligations that come with it.

Overview

Although from a day-to-day perspective business entities can be simple, they have complex contours. This book is organized into four parts. The first part, Chapters 1 and 2, lays the groundwork for the rest of the book. It explores the kinds of risks freelancers face and explains the pros and cons of doing business without a legal entity—that is, as a sole proprietorship. It also introduces some basic ideas about business entities, including what they are, how they are formed and organized, and how they are managed.

In the second part, Chapters 3 and 4, we'll jump into an overview of the two most common legal entities that freelancers will want to consider as they move beyond sole proprietorships: LLCs and corporations. We'll explore the potential advantages of these business types, as well as the nuts and bolts of forming and managing them.

The next part, in Chapters 5 through 9, dips into a few broad topics that apply to forming and operating a business using a legal entity. For many freelancers, limited liability will be one of the significant motivations for forming a legal entity. Chapter 5 looks at the *limits* of the protections offered by LLCs and corporations. Chapters 6 through 8 provide a short introduction to technicalities associated with business names, taxes, and contracts. Finally, Chapter 9 brings together the book's main ideas to give you a framework for thinking through your business structuring decision using all that you've learned in your reading. It includes a chart comparing the features of the different business forms discussed in the book, as well as some guidelines to help you get your thoughts in order.

The book's last chapter is for freelancers who are thinking about going into business with a colleague or two as one of several business structuring options. This chapter covers a couple entity types that aren't covered elsewhere and briefly introduces some of the concerns that arise in business partnerships.

A short glossary closes out the book. The glossary is a quick reference for the sometimes confusing terminology of business law. Although the glossary repeats some of the information in the main text, it also goes into greater depth on a few technical topics that may come up during the process of organizing a business entity. I encourage every reader to scan through the glossary.

A Few Things This Book Is Not

I've written this book chiefly for freelancers who plan to own and operate their business as a solo operation. To keep things lean, I've deliberately minimized or omitted topics that would only muddy the waters for the average freelance business, like employment matters and finance. If you plan to have employees, as opposed to subcontractors, be sure to seek out specialized advice regarding your employer-related obligations. I assume that freelance businesses have limited financial needs. In particular, a business that will raise money from investors (people who contribute money to the business in exchange for an ownership interest in the company) needs specialized, professional advice to avoid potentially serious legal consequences.

Although there are some general principles that apply in most places, the specific rules governing business organizations still heavily depend on the state where the business is organized and the place where it does business. How a given structure will affect your business, personal assets, and finances is contingent on many factors. This book is meant to be an educational resource and isn't intended to be legal or tax advice. Fortunately, getting detailed, personalized, professional advice from a tax expert and a business lawyer needn't be expensive. There are good resources online (FindLaw.com and LegalZoom.com are just two examples) for finding qualified professionals in your state who work on a freelance and low- or fixed-fee basis. From a lawyer's perspective, freelance businesses aren't particularly complicated or unusual, so for a few hundred dollars you can get the advice you need to get your business started on the right footing. I recommend shopping around to find a professional who as part of the startup process will not just give you advice on how to organize your business, but also resources like form documents and a rundown of future governance obligations. Hopefully after reading this book you'll know the right questions to ask and will understand the answers.

The ideas we'll explore will be new for many readers. As with any technical subject, the devil of business law is always in its details. Getting familiar with the legalese can be a little overwhelming, but it's worth the effort. Just like learning how to ride a bike, learning how to operate a business takes a little patience and work. Once you're up and running, you'll find that it's a lot easier than it seemed at first glance.

Thank you for picking up this book, and good luck with your freelance business!

CHAPTER 1

Managing Risk

Decisions about how to structure your business are really decisions about how you will manage your risk. In this context, "risk" is an open-ended concept that goes well beyond the kinds of doomsday scenarios that we typically think of when we think of business risk: calamitous litigation or ruinous bankruptcy. Risk also touches on small things—mistakes in a deliverable, a missed deadline, missed tax deductions—and everything in between. When you make good management choices about your business, you are managing your risk. In this effort, forming a legal entity can be one approach among many.

To understand the benefits of forming a legal entity for your freelancing business, you first have to examine the consequences of running a business without one. The truth is that not every freelancer needs or wants to take on the added complexity of forming a legal entity for their business. Many small businesses operate without them.

Sole Proprietorships

A business operated by one person without a separate legal entity is called a **sole proprietorship**. A sole proprietorship is the simplest legal form a business can take. It requires no special legal documentation to come into existence. Rather, it arises as soon as its owner takes steps to operate as a business. **There is no legal distinction between the owner of a sole proprietorship and the sole proprietorship itself.** Lots of people are sole proprietors without realizing it: a teenaged babysitter or the dog walker you find on Craigslist are (usually) sole proprietors. Many freelancers are sole proprietors, too.

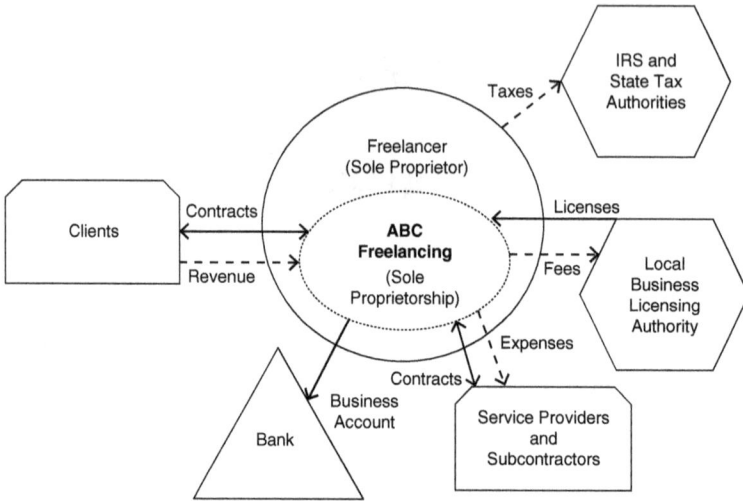

Figure 1.1 Sole proprietorship structure diagram

Figure 1.1 illustrates the interrelationship of the business owner and the sole proprietorship. Here the freelancer is doing business using a fictitious business name, ABC Freelancing. Note that the business is *inside* the freelancer's bubble: it has no separate existence apart from the freelancer. All of the business's relationships fall within the freelancer's bubble to show that the freelancer is *personally* responsible for all of it.

Operating as a sole proprietorship has several advantages over other types of business organization. Because it doesn't require any special paperwork to come into existence, it costs nothing to form. It imposes no special administrative burdens, which can take time and potentially require professional help. Although a sole proprietorship can adopt a unique name, for marketing purposes or otherwise, it can also operate using just the owner's name. This shaves a bit of cost for business licensing and avoids trademark pitfalls.

Kara the Academic Editor

Kara is an adjunct biology professor with a doctorate from a top university. Because she doesn't earn quite enough from her day job to cover her expenses, she sometimes moonlights as a freelance editor, working with academic writers in her field to improve their articles before they get submitted to graduate committees or journals for evaluation. She gets most of her work on freelancing websites, though she'll sometimes find projects through referrals.

Kara has some savings and an old car, but doesn't otherwise have much in the way of personal assets. She's never given much thought to forming a legal entity for her freelance work. For one thing, she suspects that the costs of forming an entity would consume a lot of her freelancing income. The freelancing sites she gets work through provide all the framework she needs. Legal risk has never entered her mind; as far as Kara is concerned, academics don't sue each other. Kara might conclude that she's better off operating as a sole proprietor for now.

Although they have no formal requirements to get started, sole proprietorships still need to follow certain rules and principles that apply to every business organization. Operating any business requires a business license from the county where the business is located. As part of the business licensing process, sole proprietorships that operate under a name other than the owner's also need to file a **fictitious business name statement**, which lets the public know who is behind the name. Local naming rules vary, but at minimum the name needs to be something unique; someone else can't have the name already registered with the county clerk's office.

Owners of sole proprietorships report their income and losses from the business on their personal income tax returns, by attaching IRS Schedule C, Profit or Loss from Business, to their federal returns. All the tax calculations, including deductible amounts, are done according to personal income tax rules. Unlike other business forms, a sole proprietorship can't opt to be treated as a separate taxpayer from its owner. For many freelancers, especially those who aren't sure about how much revenue they'll have, the sole proprietorship being included in personal tax returns may have little downside, and can be easier to document. But there is no way to take advantage of the special treatment that tax-regarded entities receive. Chapter 7 goes into more details about some of these advantages.

One potential disadvantage to operating as a sole proprietorship is their **perceived value**. Many people have a bias in favor of a company that's organized as an limited liability company (LLC) or corporation, seeing them as somehow more trustworthy or professional than a sole proprietorship. Although this sort of bias favors style over substance, it can be meaningful in some circles. You should think about how much this matters to you and your clients.

Outside of specific tax situations, the main downside of a sole proprietorship is that its owner bears **personal liability** for the debts and obligations of the business. Every contract the business signs, every debt it owes, and every legal liability it assumes is inseparably the owner's personal obligation. This can have serious financial consequences, especially if the business goes badly and can't pay its debts, or it gets into legal trouble. In litigation, the sole proprietor not only pays the costs of litigation out of pocket, if the case goes the wrong way the owner will also need to pay out whatever is owed to the other side of the dispute. A limited liability entity that can't pay its debts can be put into separate bankruptcy, potentially shielding the owner from serious financial harm. But a sole proprietor who can't pay the debts of their business can only turn to *personal* bankruptcy for relief, which can have disastrous consequences for the owner's private financial wellbeing. A business owner who also owns substantial personal property, like a home, car, investment portfolio, or even a valuable baseball card collection stands to lose a lot if the business involves risk.

Limited Liability

Well over a century ago, governments began encouraging people to take more business risk by devising legal entities that offer their owners **limited liability**. A business entity with limited liability, including corporations and LLCs, has a distinct existence apart from its owners and bears its own obligations. The business entity's owner is ordinarily off the hook for the vast majority of the company's debts. The company's creditors—lenders, service providers, and even people who have won lawsuits against the company—can't come after the owner's personal assets to recover what they are owed. We'll go into the limits of limited liability in Chapter 5.

Assessing Your Risk

As you begin thinking about whether to operate as a sole proprietorship or to form a limited liability entity, take stock of the risks you will face as your business grows and changes. For many freelancers, the benefits of operating as a sole proprietorship outweigh the risks, but be sure to think carefully about your situation before you reach that conclusion. To help evaluate your risk, here are a few questions to ask yourself:

- **Who are your clients?**

  Know who your clients are. It's always a good idea to put a new client's name through a Google search to see what comes up. An obvious area for caution is if a client has a reputation of treating its contractors badly. Lots of news about litigation can be another data point worth considering.

  Also think about your average client, both now and into the future. Is it an individual or a big business? A large organization with deep pockets might be more likely to take aggressive action than an individual, though the opposite can also be true (a large organization might decide it's not worth the trouble, while the stakes might be comparatively high for an individual). Freelancers who work with especially litigious clients, like lawyers, should be especially careful.

- **What stakes are involved in your field of work?**

  Consider the industry you're in and the kind of work you'll be doing. A freelancer who often drives a car for work, or does work that is inherently dangerous (either physically or legally), might face more risk than one who does not. Does your work touch upon your clients' valuable assets? A website designer who works on an e-commerce site with $100 million in annual sales has more risk than someone who designs personal blog sites with no commercial activity. Likewise for a copyeditor who works on unpublished novels by famous authors. Also think about the kind of stakes your clients face. If their stakes are high, yours are probably high also. If you work on materials related to big corporate transactions, like initial public offerings, do your deadlines factor into the deal's success? If you make a mistake, could it cost someone their job, hurt a client's profits, or damage reputations?

- **What obligations do you expect to take on?**
Freelance businesses can wind up with a lot of different types of legal obligations that can contribute to risk. Will your business carry substantial debts? Beyond loans, which you probably will have to personally guarantee anyway, think about if you plan to work with subcontractors or take on other forms of financial obligation. Even if your client doesn't pay its bill you will still owe your subcontractors for their work. Also consider the kinds of contracts you'll be signing with clients. Some clients may require contracts stuffed with onerous terms that are difficult to comply with.

- **What kinds of assets do you have to protect?**
Someone who owns a home or other substantial property (investments, other passive sources of income, real estate) makes a better target for money-motivated litigation than someone living paycheck to paycheck. Few people will sue for money if they don't have a chance of collecting; the lawyers still have to be paid even if the losing side has no means of paying a big judgment.

- **How risk-tolerant are you?**
Your tolerance for risk isn't just about the sort of assets you might lose. It also relates to your ability to weather a financial setback. A young person who rents an apartment and doesn't have much in the way of personal assets is probably less concerned about having to start over than someone who is middle-aged, owns a house, and has children. If you are nearing retirement, you are probably especially wary of exposing your savings to business risk.

- **What kind of insurance is available to manage your risk?**
Every business, regardless of its form, should carry some amount of liability insurance to avoid being wiped out by one bad mistake. Consider the kinds of activities you will undertake for your business. If you plan to drive a car as part of your freelance work, make sure that your auto insurance covers business uses. If your work takes you out of the home, consider a property and liability (P&L) policy to ensure that you're protected if you damage another person's property while you're on the job. Talking to an insurer about your business can also give you better insight into the kinds of risks

faced by people in your line of work. Like the commercials on TV say, insurers have seen just about everything. Best of all, this sort of consultation is free.

- **How do you anticipate your business growing and changing?**
  If you decide to operate as a sole proprietorship, you can always form a separate legal entity later. Perhaps your freelancing work is a haphazard side business with long stints between jobs, and the work you've been doing hasn't justified forming a legal entity. But if you anticipate your business growing, with lots of new clients and projects on the horizon, it might be a good idea to form your legal entity *before* the risks start piling up. It can be difficult to move a sole proprietorship's obligations into a new company.

Lane the Photographer

Lane is an accountant by day who sometimes earns extra money as a portrait photographer. For several years he has operated his photography business as a sole proprietorship, essentially using his income from the business to pay for upgrades to his photography equipment, which he's written off as a business expense on his tax returns.

In search of a niche that might turn his photography into a bigger source of income, Lane discovers a demand among the local extreme mountain biking scene for gnarly portraits of riders bombing down mountainsides. Even though Lane lets the riders decide for themselves how crazy they want to be, he worries about his camera causing a distracted client to crash.

Imagining lawsuits by a rider's next of kin, Lane takes a few steps to manage his risk: he starts looking into insurance that will protect him and his clients if there's an accident, he begins thinking about forming a legal entity that will limit his personal liability, and he asks a lawyer to draw up a contract for clients to sign that includes a liability waiver.

Thinking about Litigation Risk

Litigation is something you'll hopefully never face in your freelancing career. You can go a long way to avoid litigation by doing good work and fulfilling your professional obligations, especially where money is concerned. But even when you do everything right you can still get blind-sided by aggressive lawyers, and mistakes do happen. Because litigation can be an especially expensive and damaging event for a small business, it's a good idea to understand a few things about it.

First of all, if anyone ever threatens to sue you or your company, be sure to talk to a lawyer about your options before offering *any* response; even acknowledging receipt of a threatening letter can have consequences. Aggressive attorneys will threaten all manner of hellfire to recover what their client thinks it is owed. They might threaten to sue for an outra-geous sum of money, or they might assert that they can come after your personal assets even though your business is operating as a limited liabil-ity entity and the company owns all of the obligation. The goal of such threats is to scare you into making a mistake.

You may be wracking your brain trying to come up with a situation where your business would be sued. It could be that your line of work really doesn't expose you to litigation, in which case you're lucky to be able to discount this element of your risk analysis. But bear in mind that litigation can cast a wide net. You might only contribute a small part of a large project, but if a firestorm of litigation breaks out, someone—either at your client or at the company suing it—might run across your involve-ment and conclude that you should be dragged into the litigation.

Lawsuits are expensive even if you win. No matter how good your case, hiring a lawyer and paying court fees can quickly drain your busi-ness's coffers. Unethical people will sometimes file lawsuits knowing that they'll get a favorable settlement because the cost of litigation is too high for their victim to endure. This is where insurance can be helpful. A good insurance policy will cover litigation costs, sometimes with the insurer's own lawyers taking on the case. In these cases, insurers are protecting themselves from making a big payout, so they don't necessarily have your best interests at heart. But at least they're picking up the tab.

A threatening letter doesn't mean you've been sued. To initiate a law-suit, someone has to take the step of filing paperwork in a court and providing you with **service of process**. Many businesses don't know that they've been sued until a process server shows up at their door with official paperwork. Among the documents the server delivers will be a copy of the **complaint** the person or business suing you, called the **plaintiff**, has filed against your business. The complaint describes the technical particulars of what the plaintiff thinks your business has done wrong, and sets out the plaintiff's demands. A plaintiff's demands might include a sum of money, or that the court order your business to take certain steps, such as delivering a final product (whether you produce it, or pay someone else to do it for you) or stopping use of the plaintiff's intellectual property.

A lawsuit rarely goes all the way to trial, simply because it's too expensive. Your lawyer may advise you to enter into a **settlement agreement** to end the lawsuit. To stick, a settlement might require your company to pay part of what the plaintiff has demanded, or take other actions. The good thing about a settlement agreement is that you can stop the bleeding from legal fees, and you can have some say about how much your company has to pay. The downside, of course, is that you might have to pay something to settle, even though you don't think you're at fault.

If a lawsuit does go all the way through to trial and your opponent wins, what then? The trial moves into the **remedies** phase, where the court determines whether to order your company to take certain actions and pay some money to make the plaintiff whole. Once the plaintiff has a court order against your company, it becomes a creditor of your business. If you're a sole proprietorship, the winning plaintiff can now take harsh steps, like putting a **judgment lien** on your property (such as your house or car). If your company is a limited liability entity, the plaintiff might be limited to going after just the company's property. For a freelance business that might not amount to much: the cash in the company's bank account, maybe some equipment you've expensed. In Chapter 5 we'll look at one theory a plaintiff might use to try to reach past your limited liability entity to get at your personal assets. Fortunately, overcoming a properly managed legal entity's liability protections isn't easy.

Many businesses have started to manage litigation costs by requiring their contractors to agree to resolve disputes through **binding arbitration** instead of litigation. Arbitration is intended to be a "light" version of litigation, with fewer technicalities and shorter processes leading to a result that is comparable to that of litigation. Because it's relatively simple, arbitration can involve lower legal fees and get resolved more quickly. As arbitration has grown in popularity it has also grown in complexity, meaning it's still an expensive process.

The Worst Case Scenario: Bankruptcy

If you reach a point where your business is deeply underwater, creditors are harassing you with phone calls and threatening letters, and you don't see a way out, **bankruptcy** offers a potential safety valve. When an individual or business declares bankruptcy, a court orders the debtor to pay what it can, usually by selling off assets, and then voids the rest of the debts. Bankruptcy itself is expensive and can have consequences for your personal finances for years afterward, so it isn't something to do lightly. But it's nice to know that it's there.

An important distinction to understand when you're still sorting out how to structure your business is the difference between **personal bankruptcy** and **business bankruptcy**. These are just the way they sound. In a personal bankruptcy, the individual debtor seeks relief. In a business bankruptcy, a legal entity is the "person" trying to escape otherwise inescapable debt. A sole proprietor has no option but to seek personal bankruptcy, because there is no distinction between the individual and the sole proprietorship. On the other hand, someone who operates a limited liability entity might be able to put just the company into bankruptcy, leaving personal assets out of the process. Bear in mind, however, that in a bankruptcy process the company's debts will be exhaustingly analyzed, and any debts that the owner has assumed will stick unless the owner separately declares personal bankruptcy. We'll look into how assumption of liability works in Chapter 5.

The United States offers debtors several flavors of bankruptcy, referred to by their chapter in the U.S. Bankruptcy Code. The two most likely to apply to a small business are Chapter 7 and Chapter 13 bankruptcies.[1] In **Chapter 7 bankruptcy**, which is available both to individuals and business entities, the court appoints a trustee to sell the debtor's assets and apportion the resulting value among the company's creditors. In a Chapter 7 business bankruptcy, all of the legal entity's assets are sold and the entity itself usually gets dissolved. In a personal Chapter 7, the debtor's personal assets get sold off. Unlike a Chapter 7 business bankruptcy, the Chapter 7

---

[1] Nolo.com is a good resource for information about Chapter 7 and Chapter 13 bankruptcies. Nolo. 2017. "Bankruptcy." www.nolo.com/legal-encyclopedia/bankruptcy (accessed August 3, 2017).

personal debtor can use **exemptions** to protect some assets from being liquidated. The exemptions are designed to prevent someone in bankruptcy from ending up penniless or unable to earn a living. The specific exemptions are dependent on state law, but usually include things like a certain amount of cash, a portion of the equity in your home, a certain amount of the value in your car, and otherwise valuable but meaningful items like wedding rings.[2] Ordinary things like clothes and household goods are usually exempted as well. Importantly, a Chapter 7 personal bankruptcy might allow the debtor to keep assets related to her business. Individuals with high net worth or very large debts might not be able to use Chapter 7 bankruptcy.

Chapter 13 bankruptcy is only available to individuals. Unlike Chapter 7, Chapter 13 doesn't force the debtor to sell off nonexempt assets. Instead, the debtor gets to reorganize her debts into a repayment plan, which gets the court's blessing. Ideally, the individual in Chapter 13 bankruptcy gets to carry on doing business as before, with a portion of future income set aside for the repayment plan.

Another type of bankruptcy you've probably heard of is **Chapter 11 bankruptcy**. Chapter 11 is an elaborate and expensive path usually followed only by large businesses or individuals with exceptionally high debt. In Chapter 11 bankruptcy, the debtor gets to reorganize its debts under a payment plan, but creditors get a say in how the plan works. It's available to both individuals and businesses, with a streamlined process available for "small business debtors" (entities with less than $2,490,925 in debt).

Needless to say, bankruptcy is a complicated knot, with overlapping layers of federal and state laws, personal and business debts, and a parade of creditors. If you take nothing else away from this brief discussion, remember that a business entity can be put into separate bankruptcy from its owner. Provided that the owner isn't also on the hook for crushing debts related to the business, a limited liability entity can take a big gob of debt into the ether, leaving the business owner free to start again.

---

[2]Kathleen Michon. 2016. "Bankruptcy Exemptions – What Do I Keep When I File for Bankruptcy?" www.thebankruptcysite.org/bankruptcy-exemptions, (accessed August 3, 2017).

CHAPTER 2

Legal Entity Basics

What Is a Legal Entity, Anyway?

If you are a sole proprietor, you *are* your business. Even if you adopt a name for your business as a branding strategy, you're just wrapping *yourself* in a label. From every meaningful perspective there's no division between a sole proprietorship and its owner.

Perhaps the most important thing distinguishing sole proprietorships from legal entities like LLCs and corporations is that legal entities have a **separate existence** from their owners. They come into being by complying with state laws, and once they're organized they are treated, in a strange way, like people. In fact, legal entities have a wide range of rights and privileges that living, breathing people enjoy. These rights and privileges are why people often speak of **corporate personhood**. Although a legal entity can't feel pain, get sick, or get thrown in jail, it can enter into contracts and own property, and even enjoys constitutional rights like free speech.

You can think of a legal entity as a fictional person who lives in a three-ring binder. A few things that go into the binder are dependent on state law and tax rules, but many of the details are left up to the business owner. It can be useful to think of legal entities as **legal fictions** because like fictional characters their qualities are largely up to the person drafting their paperwork. Many corporate lawyers earn their living shaping the "character" of their clients' business entities. The right words can lower your tax bill and reduce or eliminate your personal liability. But this raises a final point about the fictive nature of business entities: even though they only exist on paper, they can have very real effects on their owners' financial wellbeing.

How Legal Entities Are Formed

Although business entities are subject to wide range of rules, from federal taxation to local licensing, they are first and foremost creatures of state law. Specifically, to exist at all, a business entity needs to be formed according to the rules set out in a state's business-related statutes. The steps required to create a legal entity depend on the form the entity will take.

Forming a legal entity requires filing paperwork and fees with a state's business regulator, typically a branch of the secretary of state's office.[1] The paperwork can be filed in person, by mail or, in some states, online. Once the entity's formation paperwork is on file, it becomes a "person," able to enter into contracts, own property, sue or be sued, and accumulate tax obligations.

Can I Form a Legal Entity Outside of My Own State?

Although you can form a legal entity in any state, it's unlikely to be a good idea for most freelancers to organize outside of their home states. Large organizations often form entities in distant jurisdictions for various reasons. For example, Delaware is a popular place to incorporate in because its corporate laws are flexible, simple, and favorable to business, especially businesses that plan to go public.

Every state requires companies that are formed elsewhere and do business within the state to register as a foreign business entity. Such registrations cost money, both at the time of filing and on an annual basis. These are in addition to the fees to maintain the company in the state where it is organized, which probably will include a special service fee paid to a local service agent to accept service of process on behalf of the company. Depending on your situation, there can also be tax consequences for being located, or simply working or selling products, in multiple states. These costs aren't likely to make sense for a freelance business that otherwise might want to take advantage of some legal

---

[1]Massachusetts, Pennsylvania, and Virginia refer to their secretary of state as the secretary of the commonwealth.

technicality available in another state's laws but not available where the freelancer lives. Of course, freelancers who work in multiple states, such as those who split time between two homes, will need to address this issue to stay in compliance. If you think you may be subject to more than one state's rules, it might be helpful to talk to a legal professional to find out what's involved.

Getting Organized

Organizing a legal entity involves more than just submitting paperwork with the state. It also requires attending to the formalities of **governance**. Each kind of legal entity has a different set of formal requirements, determined by state laws and the company's organizing documents. Some of these arise when the company is formed, while others crop up over the course of the business's existence. Some, such as business licenses and periodic reports, are public documents that get filed with local and state authorities. Others, like the company's operating rules and business records, are kept private. Taken together, the formation documents and the ongoing governance documents form the "person" of the legal entity. We'll take a detailed look at how these things work for limited liability companies and corporations in the next two chapters. For now, it's worth looking at a few ideas that apply across the board.

- **Documenting approvals**

  Newly formed business entities customarily need the approval of their owners or management to complete the organization process. This might include approving the owner's initial investment in the company, the appointment of a manager or officers, or establishing the company's tax year. Documenting these formal approvals is important to ensure that no one can question the validity of the company's formal organization. You don't want to skip this step only to discover that you have been signing contracts on behalf of your company without having given yourself the right authority. Some organizations accomplish these approvals with meetings, while a freelancer is probably going to use **written consents** instead.

- **Documentation of ownership**

  The ownership of a legal entity needs to be carefully documented. In some cases, evidence of ownership may be integrated into the company's organizing documents. In others, it gets written down in a simple document that sets out basics like what the owner owns (say, 100 shares of stock, or 100 percent of an LLC's membership interests) and how much it's worth. If your state requires companies to issue a physical representation of ownership, there's no need to buy fancy certificate paper unless you'd like something to hang on your wall. Ordinary paper works just fine.

- **Business licenses and local tax registrations**

  Every business needs to hold a license issued by local authorities, usually the county where the business operates. Some cities impose additional licensing or tax rules for businesses operating within city limits. The new entity will need to hold its own licenses and registrations. If you already have a business license for your sole proprietorship you will need to get a new license for the legal entity. Depending on the rules of your jurisdiction, you may want to cancel your old business license, or allow it to lapse. **Be sure to understand local requirements before making any business structuring decisions.**

Keeping Up the Fiction: Corporate Separateness

Respecting the separate existence of a legal entity is vitally important for preserving its liability protections and avoiding tax problems. Intermingling personal and business assets is awfully easy to do when you are the only person involved in a business. Maintaining the distinction between your personal and business matters takes a little effort, especially when the company is first getting organized, but it's important.

The following important steps are necessary to preserve separateness. If doing these things ever starts to feel tedious or inefficient, remember that they are all helping to *maintain a legal fiction*. The story might be dull, but it needs to be complete to do its work.

- **Separate money matters**

  Mixing personal and business finances is one of the cardinal sins a business owner can commit, even as a sole proprietor. This is because the Internal Revenue Service (IRS) can use mixed finances as an excuse to disallow deductions for *all* business expenses paid out of a mixed account, on grounds that the deductions were personal expenses. For an owner of a legal entity, mixing finances can also undermine the owner's liability protections. To avoid these expensive pitfalls, every business needs to have its own bank account, preferably at a separate bank from the owner's personal accounts. It should also have its own cash management tools if the business needs them, such as a separate account with an online payment service (such as PayPal or Venmo) and a separate credit card, if your business needs one.

- **Separate financial records**
  In addition to keeping scrupulous records of the company's earnings and expenses paid from its own account, including receipts and other documentation, the owner needs to track any costs the owner incurs on behalf of the company as a reimbursable expense. For example, a freelancer might buy office supplies using her personal credit card and later reimburse herself through a transfer from the company's account to her personal account. Both the purchase of the supplies, with receipts, and the expense reimbursement should be recorded on the company's books. This not only avoids a question of intermingling funds but it also avoids the reimbursement being treated as salary that is subject to income and employment taxes. Ideally, the business avoids this problem by buying supplies using its own cash.

- **Separate assets**
  The company should own the equipment and supplies that it needs to run the business, and the owner should avoid using these assets for personal purposes. If the business requires a computer, ideally the company owns a separate machine from the owner's personal computer. This will let the business deduct more of the computer's cost as a business expense, and ensures that the owner's personal computer doesn't inadvertently end up being treated like an asset of the business if the company gets into financial trouble. Making too much personal use of business assets is one way creditors can show that you aren't treating the business as separate from yourself, which can undermine your legal entity's limited liability protections. We'll get into this more in Chapter 5.

- **Compliance**

  Keeping the company in compliance with state and local laws is crucial. Compliance means filing required reports, fees, and taxes when they are due, maintaining business licenses, and documenting any required corporate governance procedures. Most jurisdictions mail out reminders of important reporting and licensing deadlines, but it's always a good idea to keep these dates on your business calendar. If your company needs to go through some internal motions to satisfy state law rules, such as the annual re-election of a corporation's director, you'll need to remember to document those actions.

- **Recordkeeping**

  The business entity's formal records (state and local filings and reports, written management approvals, business licenses, and so on) should be kept together in a **minute book**. The minute book can be a binder or a file folder. Some states still require companies to retain original hard copies of certain things, but it can also be useful to keep digital copies of everything, in case someone (a bank or credit card company, for example) asks for an electronic copy of a business record.

- **Adequate capitalization**

  The company should have sufficient funds available to it to pay its debts as they come due. Funds can be in the form of capital held by the company in a bank account, or as a reserve of funding such as a line of credit or an explicit obligation of the owner. Be careful about the last option: it can be treated as a personal guarantee that gives rise to personal liability.

  What "adequate capitalization" means in practice depends on many factors, including the type of obligations the business has, the standards appropriate to the company's field, and state-specific rules, but the amount is generally much smaller than you might think; a business doesn't literally have to have cash on hand to pay for every conceivable debt it might face. Many states measure adequate capitalization at the time the company is first organized, when it has no assets. In states that follow this rule, it can be enough to deposit a small sum of money (say, $10) into the business's bank account as consideration for ownership in the business. Other states may have stricter rules that expect businesses that take on substantial risk to have taken steps to manage that risk, whether by having cash on hand, a source of financing available, insurance, or a combination of these.

- **Visibility**
  The legal entity needs to be the public face of the business. Its name should appear on stationery, business cards, and other promotional materials. The legal entity also needs to be the "person" entering into contracts related to the business. We'll get into contracts in Chapter 9.

The good news about corporate separateness is that it needn't take up a lot of time once it is part of your normal routine. Get into the habit of treating your company as something separate from yourself, and in no time it will be second nature.

Financing and Ownership

When you form a legal entity you become its owner. A few important ideas intersect with ownership, including how the business will be financed. Most freelancers will have to spend some of their own money on their business's expenses, especially in the beginning when the company doesn't have any revenue. Some may also want to explore taking out a loan for large expenses like equipment or training. Let's look at a few legal considerations about how these forms of financing work.

Debt

Debt financing is exactly what it sounds like: taking out a loan from a bank or a supportive individual, with a contractual obligation to pay back the borrowed money at a future time. When it comes to debt, remember that your interest payments to an outside lender are probably deductible business expenses at tax time. It's always a good idea to document a loan arrangement, even if it's with someone close to you, so both sides are clear about the basics of the deal, like how much interest will be paid, how often payments are to be made, and how long you will have to pay back the principal. It also protects both your business and the lender in case something goes wrong.

If you don't have a rich uncle to lend you money for your business, but you need some operating cash, you can always try getting a small business loan from a bank. Even if your business will be housed in a limited liability entity, and that entity will be the borrower, a bank that lends to a newly formed small business entity will always look to the entity owner's personal assets and credit history to make its lending decision, and will require the owner to personally guarantee the loan. We'll look at some of the consequences of personal guarantees in Chapter 5.

Equity

Equity is shorthand for the amount of money or other valuable assets that the business's *owners* contribute to it. Usually, the personal liability of an owner of a limited liability entity is limited to the amount she has contributed to the company as equity; in other words, what you put into your company becomes the company's property and can be lost if the company fails. In a freelance business, the most likely approach will be to treat everything the freelancer contributes to the company—cash, equipment—as an equity contribution. You might have also heard of "sweat equity," which refers to the uncompensated time a business owner puts into making a business a success. Unfortunately, sweat equity isn't the sort of thing that gets counted on a company's books. It's the price of building a successful business.

A legal entity keeps track of its owner's equity in what accountants call a **capital account.** The capital account changes as the owner contributes money to the company, the company's balance sheet changes, or the company distributes money to the owner. The capital account of a company owned by one person is relatively easy to deal with, since the owner has 100 percent of everything. For now, the important thing to remember is that the money you put into or take out of your business needs to be carefully recorded. It factors into your company's substance as a separate entity and is important at tax time.

In theory, a business can raise capital by selling ownership interests to outside investors. You should approach financing your business this way with a great deal of caution. With ownership comes control. Sorting out how much say the investor will have over the direction of your business is not always easy. A lawyer will almost certainly be needed to protect yourself and your business. By the time the lawyer has put together an investment agreement, sorted through changes to the company's governance documents to reflect the new ownership structure, and complied with federal and state securities laws, you might have been better off just borrowing the money you needed.

CHAPTER 3

Limited Liability Companies

Pros and Cons of Limited Liability Companies

Pros

- Cheap to form and maintain.
- Relatively few governance formalities.
- Limited liability for owner.

Cons

- State tax treatment may be unfavorable.
- Liability protections might be easier to breach than a corporation's.
- More expensive to form and manage than a sole proprietorship.

The limited liability company, or LLC, has become a popular legal entity choice for small businesses in many fields. The reason for the LLC's popularity is simple: it offers business owners limited liability at low cost. It is also easy to operate, with very few mandatory requirements. Wyoming adopted the first LLC statute in 1977, but it was not until the late 1990s that the IRS clarified that it would allow LLCs to elect for themselves whether or not to be treated as separate taxpayers from their owners. As a result of the clarified tax rules, the number of LLCs in the United States exploded.[1]

---

[1] As with all legal entities, the laws governing limited liability companies vary widely from state to state. The Revised Uniform Limited Liability Company Act of 2006 has been adopted in several states (California, District of Columbia, Florida, Idaho, Iowa, Nebraska, New Jersey, Utah, and Wyoming) and is the basis for the information in this chapter. National Conference of Commissioners on Uniform State Laws. 2006. *Revised Uniform Limited Liability Company Act.* www.uniformlaws.org.

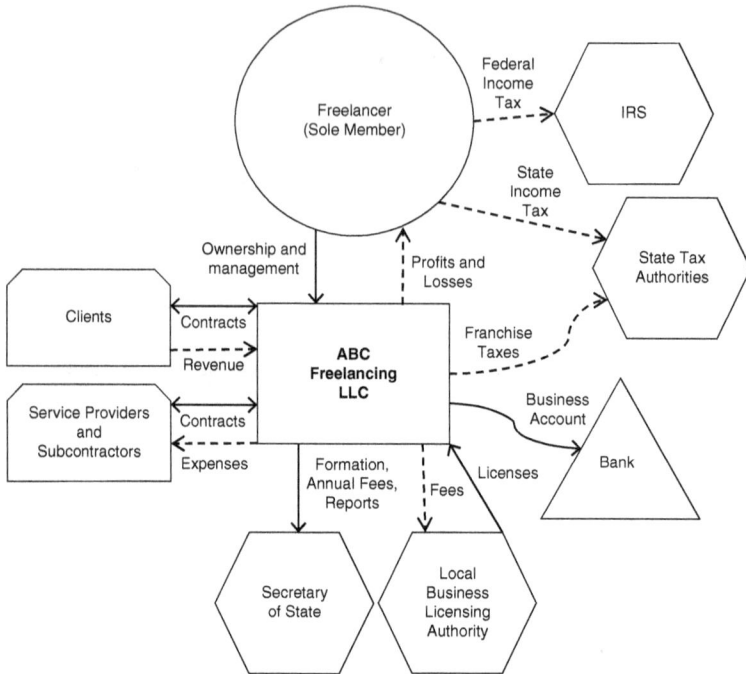

Figure 3.1 Limited liability company structure diagram

Figure 3.1 shows an example organization structure for an LLC. In Figure 3.1 the LLC is following default tax treatment and is not subject to separate income tax. Note that revenue and expenses flow through the company and end up as components of the freelancer's personal income tax calculations. The company itself doesn't have a relationship with the IRS *as an income taxpayer*, though its owner submits an extra form with the owner's personal tax returns. Meanwhile, contracts and other obligations remain with the company.

Limited Liability

The owner of an LLC is referred to as the company's **member**. Single-member LLCs are common. Members own **membership interests** in the company. Unlike the stock of corporations, an LLC's membership interests usually do not need to be paid for in cash to be legally valid. Instead, in the company's organizing documents the member can specify how membership interests are issued and held.

The member's personal liability for obligations of the LLC is limited to the amount the member has contributed to the company. Essentially, this means that all other formalities being met, the member's investment in the company is the only thing at stake should the company be sued or is otherwise unable to pay its debts.

Paul Loses His Shirt, but Keeps His House

Paul is a semiretired freelance website designer who owns Nice Site Designs LLC. When he formed his company, he specified in its organizing documents that he would become the sole member of the company in exchange for $10 in cash. Any other contributions he made to the company would be recorded as surplus capital contributions. Paul wrote a personal check for $10 and deposited it into the company's new bank account. He also used his own money to buy a new computer and software, spending a total of $5,000, which he claimed as deductible expenses of the business at tax time. Paul is assiduous about keeping up with all the formalities of his company.

A client sues Nice Site Designs LLC for damages arising from mistakes Paul made in a website's security. Fortunately for Paul, the court doesn't let the client come after Paul's substantial personal assets (his retirement accounts and home) even though he made mistakes. Unfortunately, the damages are much more than Paul bargained or prepared for, totaling over $500,000.

When the client goes to collect on its judgment against Nice Site Designs LLC it discovers that the only assets the company has are what Paul has put into it. Paul stands to lose his $10 initial contribution as well as whatever value remains in the computer and software, which are subject to being taken by the client. Ultimately, the judgment probably means that Paul's business will have to shut down, potentially through a bankruptcy process to formally wipe out the debt owed to the client. (In most states, an LLC that is *insolvent*—that is to say, it has debts greater than its assets—cannot be legally dissolved other than by a court.)

In this admittedly unrealistic scenario, the real loser is the client, who has suffered serious harm as a consequence of Paul's mistakes. In real life, a client that stands to lose this much value in a transaction with a freelancer will require the freelancer to carry professional liability insurance to protect it against such an event.

Formation

Forming an LLC is usually a simple process, started by filing a **certificate of organization** (alternatively called a certificate of formation or articles of organization) with the state's business registrar, together with a fee. The certificate of organization is a public record. The filing is usually completed in person or by mail, but many states offer online filing as well. The fee is usually between $100 and $300. Once filed, the state stamps the document or issues a separate certificate with the filing's effective date and the company's unique file number, which you'll use for all your future correspondence with the state regarding the company. Typically, the date the certificate of organization is received by the state becomes the date of formation of the company, though without paying a fee to expedite the filing's return it can take anywhere from 1 week to a couple of months to receive formal confirmation, depending on how quickly the office processes them. Some states are notoriously slow about processing filings that aren't submitted on an expedited basis.

Many states provide preprinted forms for the certificate of organization on their website. Each state has its own requirements for what information is required. Figure 3.2 shows what a completed certificate of organization might look like for a California LLC. The following items are typical:

- **The name of the business**
  There are relatively few restrictions on how an LLC is named. States usually require companies' names to include an appropriate suffix (LLC, Limited Liability Company, Ltd.) and have a few minimal restrictions. We'll cover naming in Chapter 6.
- **The company's business purpose**
  Many states require new LLCs to include a statement about what the new business will do. Some states allow an open-ended statement

Secretary of State **Articles of Organization** Limited Liability Company (LLC)	**LLC-1**

IMPORTANT — Read Instructions **before completing this form.**

Filing Fee - $70.00

Copy Fees - First plain copy free; Additional copies: First page $1.00 & .50 for each attachment page; Certification Fee - $5.00

Important! LLCs may have to pay an annual minimum $800 tax to the California Franchise Tax Board. For more information, go to https://www.ftb.ca.gov.

This Space For Office Use Only

1. Limited Liability Company Name (See Instructions – Must contain an LLC ending such as LLC or L.L.C. "LLC" will be added, if not included.)

ABC Freelancing LLC

2. Business Addresses

a. Initial Street Address of Designated Office in California - Do not list a P.O. Box	City (no abbreviations)	State	Zip Code
1234 Main Street	Anytown	CA	12345

b. Initial Mailing Address of LLC, if different than Item 2a	City (no abbreviations)	State	Zip Code
P.O. Box 54321	Anytown	CA	12345

3. Agent for Service of Process

Item 3a and 3b: If naming an **individual**, the agent must reside in California and Item 3a and 3b must be completed with the agent's name and complete California street address.
Item 3c: If naming a California Registered **Corporate Agent**, a current agent registration certificate must be on file with the California Secretary of State and Item 3c must be completed (leave Item 3a-3b blank).

a. California Agent's First Name (if agent is **not** a corporation)	Middle Name	Last Name	Suffix
Ima	Magnifique	Freelancer	

b. Street Address (if agent is **not** a corporation) - **Do not list a P.O. Box**	City (no abbreviations)	State	Zip Code
1234 Main Street	Anytown	CA	12345

c. California Registered Corporate Agent's Name (if agent is a corporation) – Do not complete Item 3a or 3b

4. Management (Select **only** one box)

The LLC will be managed by:

[ ] One Manager   [ ] More than One Manager   [✓] All LLC Member(s)

5. Purpose Statement (Do not alter Purpose Statement)

The purpose of the limited liability company is to engage in any lawful act or activity for which a limited liability company may be organized under the California Revised Uniform Limited Liability Company Act.

6. The Information contained herein, including in any attachments, is true and correct.

I. M. Freelancer

_____   _____
Organizer sign here   Print your name here

LLC-1 (REV 06/2016)

2016 California Secretary of State
www.sos.ca.gov/business/be

Figure 3.2 Example certificate of organization

such as "any business permitted under the laws of this state." Others expect a more specific description, such as "photography services." The company's stated purpose sometimes comes into play when dealing with banks, which will follow the letter of the certificate of organization. Most businesses that put limits on their scope of business in their formation document are doing so to satisfy investor requirements. Typically, freelancers will want to use the most open-ended description of their business to maximize their flexibility.

- **How the company is managed**

  Most single-member LLCs, like those freelancers are likely to use, are member managed, meaning the member has direct control over the affairs of the company. The alternative is *manager managed* LLCs, in which the company's members have appointed a specific person to operate the business. A manager is typically one of several members of the company, or an outside professional hired to do the job. These are unlikely situations for solo freelancers.

- **The name and address of an agent for service of process**

  The agent for service of process is the person who the business designates to receive formal notices from the state and service of lawsuits. The freelancer can serve as the agent for service of process, or can pay a fee to a service provider to fill this role. Because filings usually require both the name and street address of the agent for service of process, freelancers who work from home might want to hire a service to handle this requirement to keep their home address private. Some states, like New York,[2] facilitate lawsuits by requiring entities to designate the Secretary of State as the agent for service of process; in such cases, the Secretary of State forwards copies of documents served against the company to the address specified in the company's organizing document.

- **The mailing address of the company, its member, and its manager**

  Unlike the agent for service of process, the mailing address of the company usually can be a P.O. box. If you decide to use an address other than your home, be sure it is a place where you are sure to receive what is delivered. Not all states require LLCs to publicly disclose the name and mailing address of their owners, but many do.

- **The effective date of the filing**

  Some states allow filers to specify a date after the date the document is physically submitted for filing to serve as the effective date of filing. This is a good option if you have a compelling reason, such as taxes or insurance, for delaying the company's formation. Usually it makes sense to let the filing date also serve as the effective date.

---

[2] N.Y. Ltd. Liab. Co. Law § 203(e)(4).

Some states have additional requirements for completing the formation of an LLC. New York, for example, requires publication of a notice of the LLC's formation in local newspapers and a further filing to confirm that those publications have been completed.[3] In California, new LLCs must file a Statement of Information (Form LLC-12), together with a $20 fee, setting out detailed information that isn't included in the formation filing itself.[4] Instructions regarding these requirements can be found with other forms on state websites.

A certificate of organization can always be amended by filing the appropriate form and paying a fee. A common reason for amending the original certificate is to change the company's name. If you haven't chosen a name but need to form a company right away, for example to sign a risky contract, you can always form a company with a "generic" name and update it later. Once the company's name is changed you'll need to let your clients and other contractual counterparties know about the change.

Management

The Operating Agreement

LLCs have very few legally required ongoing management formalities. Some states require an LLC member to enter into a governing document, called an **operating agreement** (also sometimes called an LLC agreement). Even in states that allow LLCs to operate without operating agreements, it is usually a good idea to adopt one. Otherwise the state's default rules will apply. Depending on your situation, the default rules might not be the best fit for your business. By adopting a personalized operating agreement, you can decide for yourself how much formality you want to take on. Most freelancers will want to opt out of all but the minimal requirements that are necessary to maintain the LLC as a going concern.

The contents of a company's operating agreement are largely up to the member, provided that the state's statutory requirements are met. Every state requires different things to be included in an operating agreement, so it is important to use a form that is consistent with current state requirements.

---

[3]N.Y. Ltd. Liab. Co. Law § 206(a).
[4]Cal. Corp. Code § 17702.09.

That said, these are fairly boilerplate documents. Simple forms of operating agreement tailored to every state's laws can be found online, for free or for a fee. An experienced business lawyer should be able to provide a document tailored to your business and personal needs at nominal cost.

The operating agreement is a private document, meaning it isn't filed with the state. Some service providers, especially those entering into a financial relationship with the company (banks, insurance companies), will need to see a copy of the operating agreement as part of their new client screening process or to confirm your authority to sign documents on behalf of the company.

Once adopted, an operating agreement can always be amended, either by a signed document that describes the amendment, or by adopting a whole new agreement. The member of the LLC needs to sign the amendment for it to be effective. Assuming that the original operating agreement is properly drafted, amendments are pretty unlikely to be necessary for a freelance business.

Operating agreements typically cover the following matters:

- **The powers of the member**
  Even though an LLC has only one member, the member's authority to act on behalf of the company (sign contracts, open bank accounts, appoint officers) might need to be spelled out in the operating agreement. Many states allow open-ended language granting members essentially unlimited authority to act on behalf of their LLCs. Other states may require a more detailed list of specific authorities, which might include the power to transact business on the company's behalf, bind the company by signing contracts, borrow money and open bank accounts, and buy or sell company assets.
- **The powers of officers**
  If signing contracts with the title of "member" isn't appealing to you, you can give yourself a different title (president, for example) for purposes of day-to-day work. Be sure to document your extra titles and their authorities. Almost all the powers held by the member as member manager can be duplicated in an officer position. Your authority as member will still be necessary for formal

actions like winding up the company, making amendments to the operating agreement, or complying with requirements of banks or government authorities, but the officers of an LLC can do almost everything else, like signing contracts.

- **How ownership of the company works**

  The operating agreement determines what members can do with their membership interests, as well as how new membership interests get issued. These provisions needn't be complicated in a single-member LLC. If you later decide to bring in another member, you will probably amend your operating agreement to restrict the ability of you and your partner to sell or give away ownership interests in the company.

- **What happens to the company if the member dies, is incapacitated, or declares bankruptcy**

  Disaster planning is part of managing business risk. Unlike a corporation, an LLC can be organized to automatically dissolve at the death of its sole member. Alternatively, the company can continue to exist, with the membership interests simply becoming another asset of the former member's estate. Similar provisions addressing member bankruptcy usually only appear in LLCs with more than one member, but watch out for such terms if you're relying on a form agreement found on the Internet. Before adopting any provision that gets triggered by a disaster event, it is worth understanding if there are significant downsides. For example, how your state treats business assets in an estate, and how a dissolved business's liabilities might pass on to your heirs. If the company dissolves upon your death, its limited liability protection may go with it, leaving your heirs exposed to your outstanding business debts. On the other hand, leaving an unwanted business entity in place can add an extra layer of complexity to estate management. These are probably more important considerations for freelancers with especially valuable business assets and debts.

Ownership and Member Contributions

The rules governing LLC ownership are fairly permissive with respect to the way ownership is issued. When an LLC is organized, the operating agreement can simply state who the member is without requiring the member to pay anything for owning the company. Although paying for ownership isn't always required, it's still necessary for the LLC to be *adequately capitalized*, a topic we touched on in the last chapter. Be sure to keep track of the money you put into the company on your capital account.

If the operating agreement includes any formalities governing the issuance of membership interests, they should be closely followed. For example, the operating agreement may require the member to sign a resolution approving the issuance. If the operating agreement requires the company to issue a paper certificate of the membership interests, then that certificate needs to be prepared, signed, and kept in a safe place. A **membership interest certificate** can be an ordinary piece of paper with standard language on it, so this needn't be a complicated step provided you have a template that meets your state's requirements. If allowed by state law it's a good idea to make such certificates optional, so you needn't create one unless the need arises.

Statutory Filings and Other Maintenance Formalities

Aside from any governance requirements included in the operating agreement, the following items are often needed to keep an LLC in good standing with state and local authorities:

- **Periodic reporting**
  Most states require LLCs to file periodic reports with the Secretary of State, typically annually and usually with a small fee in the range of $25, though they can be substantially more. Illinois, for example, collects a $250 fee for annual reports filed by mail (more for electronic filings).[5] Annual reports typically call for updated information about the company, such as any change of address, change of member, or other details. They can be filed by mail and sometimes can be filed electronically. In a few states, like New York and Texas, the Secretary of State doesn't collect annual reports from

---

[5] Office of the Illinois Secretary of State. 2017. "LLC Annual Report." http://www .cyberdriveillinois.com/departments/business_services/annual_reports/llc_ instructions.html.

LLCs. Instead, those states gather information through the state tax authority.

- **Franchise and income taxes**

  Many states impose a flat tax on every legal entity registered in the state, independent from income taxes. The amount of the tax varies widely. Some states charge a flat fee across the board, while others base the fee on the company's revenue from the prior year. A single-member LLC does not file separate income tax returns. Instead, its owner reports business income and losses on IRS Schedule C, the same form used by sole proprietors. Chapter 7 goes into more detail about tax matters.

- **Local business licensing and registrations**

Formal Business Records

The simplicity of managing an LLC extends to the way the company's actions are documented. In a member managed LLC with a sufficiently permissive operating agreement, the member can mostly manage the affairs of the company without constantly documenting the member's approval in written consents or in meeting minutes. There are a few exceptions that may arise where the member's approval of the company's actions needs to be formally recorded. Even for a single-member LLC, it is important that such approvals be documented and filed with the company's records. This can feel unintuitive at times, because the sole member is often authorizing herself to act. But the absence of such formalities can be a bad fact in litigation or in an IRS audit, so it's important to follow them.

State laws rarely require LLCs to pass member resolutions as part of their routine governance process. There are certain events that do require member consents, but these are rare: selling off all the company's assets or sales of membership interests are two examples. Instead, most demands for special resolutions will come from sophisticated counterparties you will do business with, especially banks. You should expect to receive a template resolution from these sorts of businesses, so you won't have to figure out the magic phrases they're looking for. Just be sure to carefully review any form documents to ensure that they accurately reflect the deal and your company's details, such as its name and mailing address.

Kara Goes Corporate

After a few years operating her academic editing business as a sole proprietorship, Kara's circumstances have changed. She has found a permanent professorship that has allowed her to settle down and buy a home. Her editing business has also expanded. She still edits papers for academics, but now her main client is a large consulting firm that produces environmental impact reports for large-scale infrastructure projects. Her client hires her on a project-by-project basis, using a contract drafted by the client's legal team. The contract gives Kara a lot of obligations she's never faced in the academic world, like confidentiality, arbitrary mechanisms that can reduce her fees if she fails to meet certain obligations, and an ambiguous clause that might require her to carry expensive professional liability insurance. Kara is willing to take on these burdensome requirements because the client pays top dollar.

One afternoon she gets a call from her client asking her to take on a new project. During the conversation, her contact tells her that the company is in the middle of a big lawsuit over omissions in the last report Kara worked on. Although the mistakes weren't Kara's fault, the news gives her pause. She decides that it's time to think about getting insurance and forming a limited liability entity for her business.

After looking at the costs and requirements for LLCs and corporations in her state, Kara decides that an LLC is the best fit for her business needs. She likes the simplicity of the LLC's corporate governance rules, and is satisfied that the LLC will provide her with a reliable degree of liability protection if she gets caught in a lawsuit. She concludes that the extra paperwork she'll need to complete, the franchise taxes she'll have to pay, and the annual reporting she'll have to do are all small costs compared to the risks the entity will help her manage. Kara doesn't stop there, though. She also starts hunting around for professional liability insurance to see whether she can find something that will protect her at a justifiable cost, and better comply with her client's expectations.

Once Kara gets her new LLC up and running, she lets her client know that her company will own the relationship going forward. The client tells her that they can't agree to transfer her old contracts to the new company, but that in the future they'll happily prepare new contracts using her company's name.

CHAPTER 4

Corporations

Pros and Cons of Corporations

Pros

- Still fairly to cheap and easy to form and maintain, though potentially more expensive than LLCs.
- Clearly defined limited liability for owner.
- May have perceived value for marketing purposes.
- Can have tax advantages at the state level.

Cons

- Compared to LLCs, more paperwork to form.
- More formal governance requirements.
- Can have higher tax costs.

Another common business form for small businesses is the **corporation**. The idea of the corporation has a long history, extending back to before the colonial era. In the United States, corporate statutes granting business owners limited liability first came on the scene in the final years of the 19th century. The proliferation of corporations in the 20th century was accompanied by a swirl of related legal developments, from transformative regulations like those adopted following the 1929 stock market crash, to the complex and often subtle evolution of judicial rulings in specific cases brought by corporate shareholders. This long legal history is one of the reasons the corporation has conventionally been a popular form for sophisticated businesses: stable legal rules mean corporations are a more reliable way to manage risk.

Like an LLC, a corporation is formed by registering with a state government and grants limited liability to its owners. Compared to LLCs, corporations are more complicated to organize and involve more formalities. Also, fees associated with corporations tend to be higher than for LLCs, though some states have started piling on LLC fees to encourage more businesses to use corporations instead.

So why would a small business owner choose a corporation over an LLC? There are several possibilities. One is taxes. Both state and federal law may allow corporations to deduct certain expenses that are not deductible for LLCs or their members, even if the LLC elects to be treated as a corporation for tax purposes. State franchise taxes also can be lower for some corporations than for LLCs. Finance can be another reason to use a corporation. A business that plans to raise operating capital through an investor, rather than by borrowing, might be advised by an attorney to take advantage of the well-established rules governing corporate stock and the limited role of corporate owners. Still another reason to favor a corporation might be the way your state's laws treat the limited liability of corporate shareholders as compared to members of LLCs. Due to corporations' relatively long history compared to LLCs, it might be easier in some states for creditors to look past an LLC than a corporation in some situations, though this issue is rapidly fading away as the legal landscape around LLCs matures. Finally, you may conclude that a corporation just looks more professional. In some circles the branding impression of having "Inc." instead of "LLC" after your company's name can be worth the extra cost and hassle.

The bottom line is that the good reasons for a freelancer to favor a corporation over an LLC will tend to be specific to that freelancer's state rules and business structure. What follows is a basic introduction to how corporations work. If your tax adviser, accountant, branding consultant, or business lawyer suggests that a corporation will be best for your situation, this chapter will help you understand the details that go with it.

Figures 4.1 and 4.2 illustrate two potential structures for a corporation, first as a tax-regarded C corporation and then as a tax-disregarded S corporation. Note that in both figures the freelancer owner simultaneously

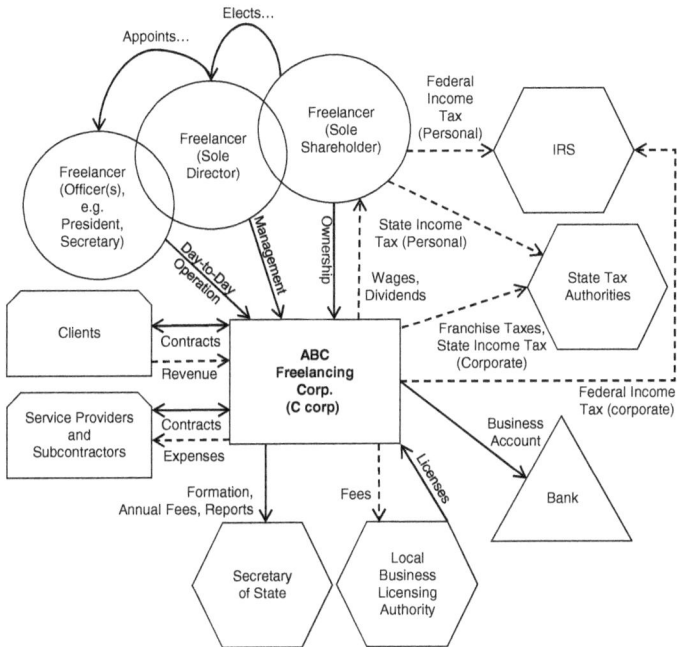

Figure 4.1 C corporation structure chart

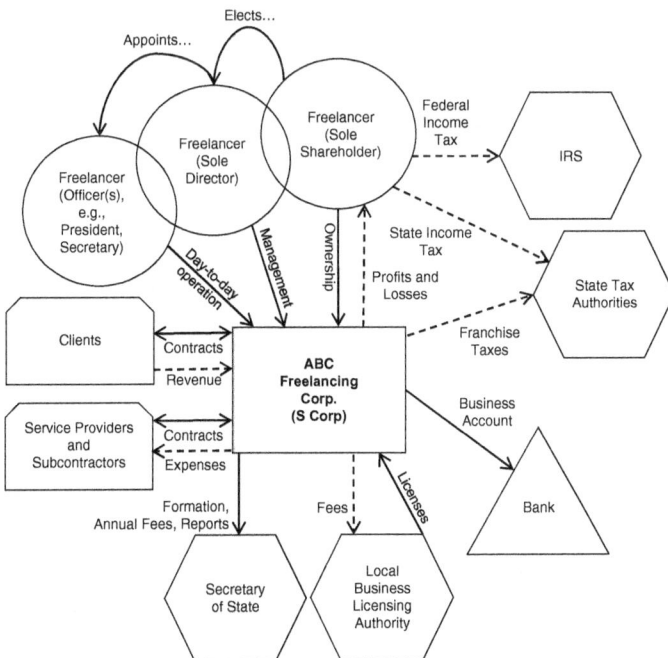

Figure 4.2 S corporation structure chart

wears every hat in the business: as the company's shareholder, director, and officer. We'll look at how these different titles work, and how the two tax variants of the corporation work, in more detail in this chapter and later in the book.

Ownership and Management

A corporation is owned by its **shareholders** (called stockholders in some states), who purchase shares of stock from the company in exchange for cash or some other valuable property. The number of shares and amount the shareholder pays per share can be nominal, such as $1.00 per share for 10 shares. The company's incorporator (for the initial issuance) or board of directors determines the value per share. Even if the purchase amount is minimal, **the shareholder must pay for the stock in a way that can be verified**, for example, by writing a personal check that gets deposited into the company's bank account.

Corporate Stock Terminology

The details of corporate stock can be pretty confusing. Fortunately, a typical freelance business can keep it simple. A freelancer's corporation is probably only going to need one **class** of stock: common stock, the default class that every corporation has. But a corporation can authorize more than one class, and each class can even have multiple **series** within it, all to give investors special privileges relative to other classes, such as dividend preferences, rights to appoint directors, and special treatment if the company goes bankrupt. A public company might have a dozen classes of stock (common, preferred A, preferred B, and so on) and the classes might even be broken down into series (preferred A-1, preferred A-2, and so on). If you ever see these terms crop up in your compliance forms, now you'll know why they're there.

A good pair of related concepts to understand is the distinction between **authorized** and **issued** shares. The number of authorized shares is set out in the articles of incorporation. It sets a limit on how many shares the corporation can *issue* to shareholders. For shares to be issued, the company needs to follow all the required formalities for issuing shares, as set out in the company's bylaws and in state law, and the shareholder buying the shares needs to actually pay for them. Once issued, the shares are said to be **outstanding**. The percentage of the *issued and outstanding shares* that a shareholder owns determines her percentage ownership of the company. In other words, if the company is authorized to issue 1,000,000 shares, it doesn't matter if you own 10 shares or 10,000 if you own all the shares that the company has issued. You are still the 100 percent owner of the company until someone else buys some shares.

The sharp distinction between a corporation's ownership and its management is one of the key differences between a corporation and a limited liability company. Unlike an LLC, which can be managed directly by its member, a corporation cannot be managed directly by its shareholder. Instead, the shareholder elects one or more members of the company's **board of directors**. A board can function just fine with a single director. The board manages the company, including authorizing important matters such as appointing officers, issuing stock, and borrowing money.

Some states require corporations to have certain **officers**, typically a president (or chief executive officer) and secretary, and sometimes a chief financial officer. Even if it isn't strictly required, you might want to appoint yourself as an officer so you can use a title of your choosing on your business card and when you sign contracts. The company's governance documents and its board of directors determine the authority of each office. Corporate officers typically have the following duties:

- A corporate **president** generally has sweeping authority to act on the company's behalf, including opening bank accounts, signing contracts, borrowing money, and managing property.
- The corporate **secretary** manages the formal records of the company, including minutes and resolutions of the board.
- A **chief financial officer (CFO)** maintains the financial records of the company. Not all states require corporations to name a CFO.

Where required, the CFO might be responsible for signing state tax documents or complying with state rules governing shareholder reporting.

One Person, Many Hats

You may be wondering why corporations are covered in a book intended for freelancers, because corporations seem to require so many different people. The answer is that **one person can successfully be a corporation's sole shareholder, sole director, and sole officer**. However, it is important to treat each role as mutually exclusive from the others. Think of the roles in a corporation like hats. The shareholder hat should only be worn when the shareholder's approval is required, such as to document the periodic appointment of directors. Likewise, the director hat should only be worn when a director approval is required, such as when called for by a bank, or to meet the state's corporate governance rules. The most commonly worn hat, by far, will be the officer hat.

Under no circumstances should you sign a contract on behalf of a corporation as its shareholder! Unlike the member of an LLC, a corporate shareholder can't be involved in the day-to-day operation of the business. That includes signing a contract *as a shareholder*. Doing so could be treated like a personal assumption of the contract's obligations, and the shareholder can be held personally liable for any obligations arising under the agreement. Avoid this by signing contracts on behalf of your corporation using your officer title.

Limited Liability

Ordinarily, a shareholder does not bear personal liability for the debts and obligations of the corporation solely by virtue of being its owner. Like the member of an LLC, a shareholder of a corporation only risks what she has contributed to the company—the amount paid for stock, plus any surplus capital contributed to the company from personal assets.

Directors and officers don't bear personal liability for the obligations of the corporation, either. The key concept to remember is that they are acting as **agents** of the corporation when they take actions on its behalf.

Directors and officers can still be held personally liable for actions they take in bad faith, or that break the law. In theory, they can also be sued by the shareholder for breaching their duty to the shareholder or the company. You aren't likely to sue yourself, but this point is worth bearing in mind if you are thinking about bringing in outside investors or directors.

Formation

A corporation is organized in several steps. Although the details of these steps can vary, a freelancer's process will probably look something like this:

1. The incorporator files articles of incorporation with the Secretary of State.
2. The incorporator signs an initial organizing resolution that provides for the incorporator's resignation from the role and can, among other things, approve the initial issuance of stock to the shareholder, including the number of shares and the price, and appoint the company's initial director(s).
3. If not already done by the incorporator, the shareholder appoints the initial director(s).
4. The initial director(s) sign an organizing resolution approving certain preliminary matters, such as the appointment of officers.
5. Complete any required postformation compliance paperwork, like publishing a public notice of the company's formation or filing information reports with the state.
6. Like any other business entity, a corporation will need its own business license and federal tax ID number.

Articles of Incorporation

A corporation is formed by filing a document called the **articles of incorporation** (or a certificate of incorporation) with a state's business regulator, typically an office under the Secretary of State. State laws vary on the acceptable method of filing. Some require an original signature on the document filed with the state, while others allow filings to be made electronically or by fax. Articles of incorporation are public records.

The articles of incorporation are signed by the company's **incorporator**. The incorporator can be the company's owner or someone helping the owner set up the company, like a lawyer or other service provider. Until the company's governance structure is put in place, the incorporator bears personal responsibility for the corporation. Essentially, the corporations' liability shield isn't working yet. It is important to take the next step in the process so the incorporator isn't on the hook longer than absolutely necessary.

A corporation's articles of incorporation include a few basic details that aren't too different from an LLC's certificate of organization. Figure 4.3 illustrates what a California corporation's articles might look like. The American Bar Association's Model Business Corporation Act,[1] variations of which have been adopted in 24 states, requires at least the following items:

- **The name of the corporation:** The limits on how a corporation is named are similar to those for LLCs.[2] A corporation generally needs to have a variation of "corporation" or "incorporated" (Corp., Inc., Limited, Ltd.) in it. See Chapter 6 for more about business names.

- **The corporation's authorized shares:** The articles must specify the number of shares of stock the corporation is authorized to issue to its ownership. Before settling on the number of authorized and issued shares, find out if they'll have a tax impact. Some states use a corporation's authorized and issued shares as a component of franchise tax calculations; authorizing ten billion shares and issuing them all to yourself for $0.00000001 per share ($100 total) might be exciting, but it could result in a *huge* franchise tax bill with no benefit.[3]

---

[1]MODEL BUS. CORP. ACT §2.02 (AM. BAR ASS'N 2016).

[2]*Id.* at §4.01.

[3]Delaware is one example of a state that calculates franchise taxes based on authorized or issued shares. A corporation can choose to use one method or the other, with corporate assets factoring into the issued shares formula. In Delaware the minimum franchise tax is $175 for corporations with 5,000 shares or less of authorized stock. Delaware Division of Corporations. 2017. "How to Calculate Franchise Taxes." https://corp.delaware.gov/frtaxcalc.shtml (accessed August 8, 2017).

Secretary of State	**ARTS-GS**
Articles of Incorporation of a General Stock Corporation	

IMPORTANT — Read Instructions **before completing this form.**

Filing Fee   –   **$100.00**

Copy Fees   –   First page $1.00; each attachment page $0.50;
Certification Fee - $5.00

Note: Corporations may have to pay minimum $800 tax to the California Franchise
Tax Board each year. For more information, go to https://www.ftb.ca.gov.

This Space For Office Use Only

---

1.   Corporate Name (Go to www.sos.ca.gov/business/be/name-availability for general corporate name requirements and restrictions.)

The name of the corporation is   ABC Freelancing Corporation

---

2.   Business Addresses (Enter the **complete** business addresses.)

a. Initial Street Address of Corporation - **Do not list a P.O. Box**	City (no abbreviations)	State	Zip Code
1234 Main Street	Anytown	CA	12345
b. Initial Mailing Address of Corporation, **if different than Item 2a**	City (no abbreviations)	State	Zip Code
P.O. Box 54321	Anytown	CA	12345

---

3.   Agent for Service of Process

Item 3a and 3b: If naming an **Individual**, the agent must reside in California and Items 3a and 3b must be completed with the agent's name and **complete** California street address.

Item 3c: If naming a California Registered **Corporate Agent**, a current agent registration certificate must be on file with the California Secretary of State and Item 3c must be completed (leave Item 3a-3b blank).

a. California Agent's First Name (if agent is **not** a corporation)	Middle Name	Last Name	Suffix
Ima	Magnifique	Freelancer	

b. Street Address (if agent is **not** a corporation) - **Do not list a P.O. Box**	City (no abbreviations)	State	Zip Code
1234 Main Street	Anytown	CA	12345

c. California Registered Corporate Agent's Name (if agent is a corporation) – Do not complete Item 3a or 3b

---

4.   Shares (Enter the **number of shares** the corporation is authorized to issue. **Do not** leave blank or enter zero (0).)

This corporation is authorized to issue only one class of shares of stock.
The total number of shares which this corporation is authorized to issue is _____ 100 _____ .

---

5.   Purpose Statement (Do not alter the Purpose Statement.)

The purpose of the corporation is to engage in any lawful act or activity for which a corporation may be organized under the General Corporation Law of California other than the banking business, the trust company business or the practice of a profession permitted to be incorporated by the California Corporations Code.

---

6.   Read and Sign Below (This form must be signed by each incorporator. See Instructions **for signature requirements.**)

_____   I. M. Freelancer
Signature   Type or Print Name

ARTS-GS (REV 12/2016)   2016 California Secretary of State
                                                                          www.sos.ca.gov/business/be

Figure 4.3   **Example articles of incorporation**[4]

- **Registered office and agent for service of process:** Just like an LLC article of organization, a corporation's article of incorporation must specify the official address of the company and the name and street address of the company's agent for service of process.

---

[4]California Secretary of State. 2017. Articles of Incorporation of a General Stock Corporation, Form ARTS-GS. www.sos.ca.gov/business-programs/business-entities/forms/ (accessed August 15, 2017).

- **Incorporator information:** The name and address of the incorporator often must be included in the articles.

For a small business, it is usually enough to satisfy the minimal requirements in the company's initial articles of incorporation, though companies can include a wide range of other items. Sophisticated companies with institutional investors often pack their articles of incorporation with dozens of technicalities regarding shareholder rights, election and powers of directors, voting, matters relating to stock, and other details. A freelance business probably doesn't need to worry about things that usually can only be changed through amendments to the company's articles of incorporation, such as procedures for electing directors, or creating special voting groups among the shareholders. One option that might be a good idea to include, if state law doesn't allow it to be included elsewhere, is a provision that allows the shareholder to take an action without holding a meeting, by signing a written resolution instead. Worst case, if a specific need arises in the future that isn't addressed in the articles as they are originally drafted, they can always be amended.

Incorporator's Resolution

After filing the articles of incorporation, the company's incorporator signs an **incorporator's resolution**. The purpose of this resolution is to allow the incorporator to resign as incorporator and, in some states, take important steps toward organizing the company. The incorporator may be allowed to authorize the initial issuance of stock to the company's shareholder, by providing for the number of shares of stock that will be issued and the amount per share the shareholder needs to pay. The incorporator may also be able to appoint the company's initial board of directors and approve the company's bylaws. By putting the company's governance structure in place, this resolution terminates the incorporator's liability for the company's debts, so it makes sense to take care of this as soon as possible after the company is formed. Lawyers usually prepare the incorporator's resolution to be signed as soon as the articles of incorporation are filed.

Shareholder's Resolution

If state law doesn't let the incorporator appoint the initial board of directors of the company, the shareholder must appoint a director as soon as possible. Until a director is in place, the shareholder can be personally liable for the company's obligations. As already mentioned, a shareholder can also be a corporation's only director, but the formal appointment needs to be documented.

Board of Directors Organizing Resolutions

Once appointed by the incorporator or shareholder, the board of directors executes a written consent approving several important details about the company's initial organization:

- Accepting the resignation of the incorporator.
- Appointing the initial officers of the company.
- Adopting the corporation's tax year, usually the calendar year.

Your business lawyer may suggest adding other details to the organizing resolutions. For example, if you intend to transfer existing assets or obligations of a sole proprietorship into the corporation, it might be a good idea to document the company's acceptance of those items in the organizing resolutions.

The company's bank will probably also require a resolution signed by the board of directors authorizing the company to enter into a relationship with the bank. Although this resolution can be included among the organizing resolutions, it is usually cleaner to handle it as a separate document. Quite often banks will provide a form of resolution for you to sign. The bank will also need to see the company's other organizing documents: its articles of incorporation and bylaws.

Postformation Compliance

Just like LLCs, new corporations often need to make disclosures or publish notices within a short time after the state accepts their formation paperwork. For example, California requires new corporations to submit an electronic report and $25 fee within 90 days, disclosing the name and address of the company's director, officers, and agent for service of process.[5] Some states, like Arizona, require corporations to publish a notice of formation in a newspaper of record.[6] Failing to comply with these requirements can cause your corporation to be dissolved or result in costly fees, so be sure to take care of them.

Securities laws and regulations are another important source of compliance requirements for new corporations. **Securities** are essentially a representation of an ownership interest in a passive investment. Because a corporate stockholder doesn't have direct management control over the company, corporate stock is a security by definition. Bonds, options, and other sophisticated financing mechanisms are also securities. Both federal and state laws impose strict requirements on the offer and sale of securities, primarily to prevent unscrupulous companies from defrauding investors. Anyone selling securities, including a new corporation, needs to comply with these regulations *or fit within an exemption to them.*

Fortunately, a typical freelance business will have no trouble finding exemptions for its initial issuance of stock, but even the exemptions can involve a little paperwork. Federal law exempts "transactions by an issuer not involving any public offering."[7] The founder of a new company can rely on this exemption without taking further steps at the federal level. Take care, though, before relying on this simple wording to issue stock to other people. Numerous regulations interpreting this simple phrase make relying on this exemption for issuances to third parties much more complicated than one might expect.

Unlike federal law, state securities laws, or **blue sky laws,** often require companies to report even the initial issuance of stock to a founder. Where required, such reports are fairly simple but often have tight deadlines and impose fees. For example, California requires small businesses to file a "Limited Offering Exemption Notice" within 15 calendar days of any issuance of a security, with a $25 fee for securities offerings of $25,000

---

[5]California Secretary of State. 2017. Statements of Information. www.sos.ca.gov/business-programs/business-entities/statements/ (accessed August 15, 2017).

[6]Ariz. Rev. Stat. § 10-203(D) (2017).

[7]Securities Act of 1933, section 4(a)(2). 15 USC § 77(d)(a)2 (2017).

or less.[8] Failing to comply with reporting obligations can expose you to penalties, so be sure to look into your obligations *before* you organize.

Are an LLC's Membership Interests a Security?

A single-member LLC can issue membership interests to its owner without worrying about securities laws. That's because membership interests in a single-member LLC that will also be managed by the member *aren't securities*. Unlike a corporate shareholder, an LLC's sole member is allowed to have direct management control over her company. Where the LLC's member will also manage the company, there isn't the passive investment component that makes corporate stock a security. Essentially, a corporate shareholder's ownership of stock is isolated under the "shareholder hat," so even if the shareholder exercises management control as the company's sole director and officer, the stock remains "passive" by definition. Likewise, bear in mind that membership interests in an LLC can be deemed to be securities if the member will not have an active role in the day-to-day affairs of the company.

Chances are good that a freelancer's corporation won't ever need to issue stock after the initial issuance. When you own all of the outstanding shares of a company there usually is little benefit to issuing more. But remember that you must comply with securities laws every time you issue or sell shares. If you plan to take on investors or sell your ownership stake to someone else, it is important to talk to an attorney about what you need to do to comply.

Management

Bylaws

Like an LLC's operating agreement, a corporation's **bylaws** set out the details of the company's management. State procedures vary on who needs to approve bylaws. The initial bylaws can often be adopted by the

---

[8]Cal. Corp. Code § 25102(f) (2017).

incorporator. Some states require them to be adopted by the shareholder or board of directors, or both. Like an LLC's operating agreement, corporate bylaws don't get filed with the state and remain private. Other than banks it's unlikely that outside parties will ask to see them. Despite being private, bylaws need to be followed as part of good governance practices. Fortunately, bylaws can be customized to minimize administrative hassles.

Although the Model Business Corporation Act *requires* corporations to adopt bylaws,[9] many state statutes make them optional. Where bylaws are optional, if the company doesn't adopt them then the state's corporate statute governs the operation of the company. Even if the default rules will work for a business, it is usually a good idea to adopt bylaws anyway. The bylaws can simply reiterate the default rules, or the incorporator can opt to depart from the norm if it will better serve the business. Even a restatement of the default rules can be helpful as a reference if a question should ever arise about how the company's management works. Here are a few provisions a freelancer might want to include, mostly to save on administrative headaches:

- If allowed by state law, eliminate notice requirements for board and shareholder meetings, or at least allow for such requirements to be waived.
- Allow shareholder and board actions to be handled by written consent instead of meetings.
- Provide that directors can be elected for the maximum term allowed by law, ideally until they resign or are replaced.
- Describe the powers of officers.
- Allow shares to be issued without creating physical share certificates.
- Provide restrictions on transferring shares, especially if the company will be owned by more than one person.

---

[9] MODEL BUS. CORP. ACT § 2.06(a) (AM. BAR ASS'N 2016).

Lucy Forms a Corporation

Lucy is a successful freelance branding professional who works with a wide range of business clients to design logos, name products, and create a wide range of promotional content. After meeting with her tax adviser, Lucy decides that forming a legal entity for her business could save her a lot of money. (We'll look at how corporations are treated for tax purposes in Chapter 7.)

She weighs forming an LLC or a corporation and concludes that a corporation is her preference. One reason for this is that her state's franchise tax regime imposes a high annual fee on LLCs that a corporation won't need to pay. Another reason is that her state's income tax rules will let her take deductions for her health insurance premiums. Finally, her branding instincts tell her that a corporation will look better as she promotes her new company within her industry.

Lucy hires a business lawyer to help her put together the paperwork for her corporation, which she decides to call Stupendous Branding Corp. The lawyer uses standard templates to prepare the company's articles of incorporation, bylaws, and organizing resolutions. These documents provide for Lucy to purchase 100 shares of the company's stock for $100 ($1 per share), an amount the lawyer recommends to give the company substance. They appoint Lucy as the company's sole director, and also name her as the company's president. Because Lucy's state requires corporations to elect directors annually, the lawyer provides Lucy with a template she can use in the first quarter each year to comply. The lawyer also puts Lucy on a mailing list to be reminded of her governance obligations at the start of each year. She puts a reminder on her work calendar, along with a reminder about the company's annual reporting deadline.

Once the company is formed, Lucy gets to work promoting her new brand. At the end of the year, she finds that her choice has paid off: her tax bill is lower, and the benefit easily covers the cost of working with professional advisers.

Formal Business Records

Just like an LLC, a corporation needs to keep its records well organized. The company's organizing documents—the articles of incorporation, by-laws, and records of director and shareholder actions—should be kept together in a binder or file, which becomes the company's minute book.

Also like an LLC, banks and other sophisticated businesses may call upon a corporation to deliver special approvals before entering into high-risk agreements with the company. Usually these are in the form of board resolutions; because shareholders don't have a management role in corporations, their approvals usually aren't needed. Situations where a board resolution is required are rare, but if they come up, the original document should be filed with the company's records and a copy given to the business requesting it.

Laws covering corporations often impose recurring governance obligations to maintain the company's good standing with the state and the authority of directors and officers to act on behalf of the business. These typically include annual statutory reports and governance resolutions. Corporate annual reports are usually pretty simple documents, requiring disclosure of the address of the business and its owner, directors, and executive officers. There is usually a filing fee of $25 or so, though it can be much more depending on how the state structures its fees. Most states have adopted an electronic filing process for these reports. Failure to submit a report on time can result in an expensive late fee and will cause the company to lose good standing with the state. If a business is out of good standing it can't file lawsuits in the state or dissolve. On a more practical level, some sophisticated clients may require their contractors to be in good standing, so falling out of good standing can have a contractual effect as well.

Although many states have stopped requiring corporations to hold **annual board and shareholder meetings** or their written equivalent, some statutes still require corporate boards and shareholders to take certain steps on a regular basis. For example, directors sometimes need to be re-elected. Some states require boards to deliver financial statements to shareholders unless the shareholders waive the requirement. A freelance business, where the same person is the shareholder and sole director, often can handle these formalities with brief, boilerplate forms. Although these resolutions never get filed with authorities, they can be important to banks or others who want to confirm the freelancer's authority to bind the corporation, and they are critically important for maintaining the company's corporate separateness.

Taxes: C Corps versus S Corps

By default, a corporation is treated as a separate taxpayer from its owner. Before it distributes profits to its shareholder, the corporation pays taxes on any income it earns, and claims deductions for any of its losses. The shareholder, in turn, must pay income tax on any distributions from the company. This is referred to as **double taxation**. A corporation subject to this default tax treatment is called a **C corporation**, often shortened to C corp.

For a solo freelancer, chances are that a tax adviser will recommend making what is called a **Subchapter S election** with the IRS. Once the election is filed, the corporation is referred to as an **S corporation**, or S corp. The IRS and state tax authorities treat an S corporation something like a sole proprietorship for tax purposes, meaning the corporation does not pay separate income taxes. Instead, the shareholder receives the company's profits and reports them on the shareholder's personal income tax return.

In some situations, staying as a C corporation can be a better deal than electing to be an S corporation. Chapter 7 goes into more detail about why this might be, and the mechanics of subchapter S elections.

A Note about Close Corporations

A few states, including California[10] and Texas[11], allow a special kind of corporation called a **close corporation**. Aside from restrictions on transferability of shares and the number of shareholders a close corporation is permitted to have (typically, up to 35), the main distinguishing feature of

---

[10]Cal. Corp. Code. § 158 (2017).

[11]Tex. Bus. Orgs. Code §§ 21.701 et seq.

a close corporation is that its shareholders are allowed to directly manage the affairs of the company without electing directors. Close corporations can often dispense with a lot of formalities of a normal corporation, such as having directors or officers, or holding regular meetings. Instead, the shareholders of a close corporation enter into a **shareholders agreement** to define their obligations to each other and to the company.

Close corporations aren't particularly popular. Drafting a shareholders agreement is a relatively complicated process, especially where more than one shareholder is involved. With complexity comes cost. Close corporations also don't typically get special advantages like lower fees or unique tax treatment. Absent a special advantage, there may be little rationale for favoring a close corporation over an ordinary C corp, S corp, or LLC.

CHAPTER 5

The Limits of Limited Liability

Formal legal entities like corporations and LLCs serve a number of purposes. They enter into contracts, own property, and can offer favorable tax treatment for some transactions. They offer multiple owners an efficient way to allocate rights. They can sue and get sued. And they also bear all of the responsibility for their obligations, whether to lenders, other businesses, or opponents in litigation. This last point—limited liability—is a significant benefit a freelancer gains by forming a legal entity.

Although limited liability sounds good at first blush, it is important to understand that this protection has boundaries. A business owner sometimes has to assume personal responsibility for a business obligation as part of a deal. An owner can also make mistakes that negate limited liability. Let's look at how voluntary and involuntary personal liability works.

Voluntarily Accepting Personal Responsibility (on purpose or by mistake)

A common way that a business owner ends up personally responsible for the debts of a limited liability entity is by **directly assuming** the company's debts. Let's look at three ways this can happen. The first way is to take on obligations as a sole proprietor before organizing a limited liability entity. The second way involves deliberately accepting personal risk for the business's obligations, through personal guarantees requested by clients or service providers. The third way involves accidental obligations that can arise from sloppy paperwork or loose talk.

Obligations Assumed before an Entity's Formation

Bear in mind that before a legal entity is formed, any actions you take on behalf of your business will be as a sole proprietor, without any limited liability protections. You continue to "own" these obligations even after a new legal entity is formed unless they can be assumed by the new legal entity. Your existing contracts will need some attention.

Some contracts may not be assignable at all. Boilerplate consumer contracts like cell phone service agreements tend to be strict on this point. You might consider letting such contracts expire at the end of their terms, so the company can enter into replacement contracts. Meanwhile, you will be personally responsible for the unassignable contracts. Be sure to account for your expenses under these business-related contracts so that their costs remain deductible.

If a contract doesn't expressly prohibit assignment, it is necessary to get the counterparty to agree to two distinct things: the **assignment** of the contract to the new company and the new company's **assumption** of the sole proprietorship's existing obligations. Sometimes your counterparties will prefer to enter into new contracts rather than assign the old one. Bear in mind that when this is done your personal obligations as a sole proprietor continue unless the new contract states otherwise. Whether it's worth fighting over this issue will depend on the circumstances. If your old contract exposed you to significant risk, it is worth fighting for assignment.

Another source of preformation liability is commitments made in the name of a legal entity that hasn't been formed. Until the entity exists it can't enter into a contract, so the person who signs on behalf of the still-unformed company becomes personally responsible. Here's an example. Ima Freelancer has submitted the paperwork to form ABC Freelancer LLC, but hasn't received confirmation of the filing yet. The paperwork was sent to the state by mail by overnight mail on June 1, so Ima assumes that the company will get organized effective June 2. Relying on that assumption, she signs a contract dated June 2, using ABC Freelancer LLC as her business name. Later she learns that a mail delay at the state capital pushed back the effective formation date of her business to June 3. From Ima's perspective, it isn't a difficult thing to document that ABC Freelancer LLC accepts the contract. The company's organizing resolutions might specifically provide for that. But asking the client to re-date the contract would look bad, so Ima decides to let it stand. If something goes *really* wrong, meaning Ima and the client are in litigation and the client's lawyers are carefully analyzing Ima's records, the client might argue that because the LLC didn't exist until the day after the contract was signed, the LLC couldn't be a party to it, and Ima should be directly responsible for the company's obligations. Even though Ima took steps to transfer her obligations to the LLC, that transfer doesn't bind the client, who never agreed to it. Of course, in real life Ima would probably have good arguments to make, such as that the client has treated the LLC as though it was the contracting party, but the point is that she could have avoided needing to make those arguments in the first place by waiting for confirmation of her company's formation before taking on obligations.

Personal Guarantees and Other Waivers of Limited Liability

Small business owners are often asked to waive their limited liability protections as part of making a deal, by agreeing to be personally responsible for their business's obligations. A new company that is owned and operated by one person won't have any credit history and probably won't have significant assets that might serve as collateral. Businesses that enter into a risky arrangement with the freelancer, such as a lender, credit card company, or equipment retailer that sells on credit, may only agree to enter into a contract with the legal entity if the owner provides a **personal guarantee** that the company will pay what it owes. A properly documented personal guarantee stands alone as a contract between the owner, the business, and the outside business. If business goes badly and the company can't pay its debts, the owner is on the hook to make up the difference. Although the business still also bears responsibility for the debt, the creditor need not bother with legal action against the business, and could take actions like placing a lien on the owner's home or car.

Formal guarantees will usually be presented as written documents, and freelancers who encounter them probably will feel pressured to accept them as part of doing business. That is especially true for businesses that need to take out loans for equipment or startup expenses. The benefit of the deal may outweigh the risk, so the personal guarantee can't be avoided.

Personal guarantees can also arise through verbal promises. A freelance photographer might say to a client, "I guarantee this will be the best photo shoot ever." Just making that promise can put the photographer on the hook for the company's obligations should something go wrong with the shoot, especially if the client has relied on the promise. If the photographer is shooting a wedding and only discovers after the ceremony that his camera's memory card was bad, the client could justifiably demand that he pay the costs to re-enact the event, and (this is the important point) threaten to sue him personally to make good on his verbal promise. Getting into the habit of putting agreements in writing, and making sure that the agreements explicitly override any verbal promises, is a good way to avoid turning loose talk in your pitch into a personal obligation.

Protecting Yourself with Merger Clauses

A good contract should include a **merger clause** (or integration clause). A merger clause provides that the contract reflects the entire agreement between the business and the client, and explicitly replaces any written or oral agreements that might have preceded it. Such a clause protects everyone involved, by ensuring that the contract is the final word on the deal. Of course, a contract with a merger clause needs to be carefully drafted to ensure that it correctly reflects the deal both sides expect. And like many legal technicalities, merger clauses might not protect a business that makes false promises or otherwise acts unethically in making the agreement. Contract law in some states provides that written contracts automatically replace preceding discussions, but even in those states it's a good idea to include it so everyone is clear about what is and isn't in the contract from the start.

Accidental Assumption of Liability

The other way a business owner can assume personal liability for a business's obligations is by not paying attention to formalities when making a deal. The client, subcontractor, or service provider needs to know that it is dealing with the company, not the freelancer in a personal capacity. A good way to do this is to have a written agreement that explicitly names the company as the responsible person. Even an informal agreement, such as an e-mail summary of the terms of a deal, can call a client's attention to the identity of the "person" it is doing business with.

Making your company's name a prominent part of your communications is a good practice. Your promotional materials—business cards, website, e-mail signature—should include the name of your company along with your name and title. If the client says something that makes you suspect that they don't know they'll be working with your company and not you personally, be sure to address the confusion.

All these steps are to avoid a mistake that is otherwise easy to make: accidentally accepting an agreement that binds you and not your company. A common way this can happen is if someone you're doing business with presents you with a contract that doesn't properly identify your company, and you agree to it without correcting the problem. Many companies have template contracts that they provide to contractors. Templates usually leave it up to the contractor to fill in their own details. Be sure to read these forms carefully and fill them in accurately, and don't sign or agree to an agreement that puts your name on the signature line without including your company's name. Chapter 8 goes into more detail about contracts.

Caroline Gets into Trouble

Caroline is a freelancing software engineer who owns Super Software LLC. Ordinarily, she handles all of her company's business using a business e-mail address (caroline@supersoftware.com), and her e-mail software always includes a signature that prominently displays her company's name and her role as the company's president. Before doing work she always gets an agreement in writing, either using a form contract her lawyer prepared for her, or using the form a client provides. But one day she lets things slip. A close friend of hers approaches her about doing work for the friend's personal injury lawyer, giving the lawyer Caroline's personal e-mail address. Caroline agrees to do work for the lawyer and, thinking this is a friendly deal, casually agrees to the terms of a contract the lawyer sends over without first looking it over. Later on, a significant flaw in Caroline's coding allows hackers to break into the lawyer's systems and steal revealing information about the lawyer's celebrity clients. As a consequence of the ensuing media outrage, the lawyer loses several clients. When the lawyer sues Caroline, she sends the case off to her company's professional liability insurance carrier. But the carrier refuses to handle the case, arguing that the contract with the lawyer doesn't belong to the company, so it isn't covered by her insurance.

Losing Limited Liability through Litigation

Even if the business owner doesn't personally assume the debts of the business, creditors can still try to go after the owner's personal assets by arguing in court that the limited liability of the business's legal entity should be ignored. Litigators call this **piercing the corporate veil**. Bear in mind that piercing the corporate veil is a *litigation strategy*, requiring the intervention of a court to be successful. It arises *after* someone has already successfully sued your business and is trying to collect.

Fortunately, courts don't like to pierce the corporate veil. For one thing, the whole idea of limited liability is to encourage business owners to take risks. If a legal entity's limited liability protections are easy to overcome, fewer people will take risks. Also, people are expected to know the risks of doing business with limited liability entities. Courts are reluctant to intervene to save someone from making a bad business decision.

Maintaining formal separateness between you and your business and not acting badly are the two most important steps for preserving the corporate veil. We looked at the steps to take to maintain corporate separateness in Chapter 2. Failing to take these steps can give rise to the idea that you have treated the business as your **alter ego**. The idea is that the owner has mingled her personal affairs with those of the business to the point that parsing them out isn't feasible or fair. Freelancers who want to rely on a limited liability entity's protections need to take this especially seriously, because businesses owned and operated by one person are more likely to fail the separateness test.

Avoiding acting wrongfully is the other important thing to do. "Wrongful" actions come in several flavors. The most straightforward are acts that are clearly unlawful, such as committing fraud or stealing. Another is acting in bad faith, by making promises that at the time you know can't be kept. At least in theory, the social contract that grants business owners limited liability doesn't allow owners to hide from responsibility for bad behavior. In practice, bad people can hire good lawyers and sometimes escape responsibility, but that's an expensive, risky, and unethical road to tread.

The most common flavor of wrongful action is **negligence**, which can ensnare even scrupulous business owners. Negligence is a failure to exercise care that a reasonable person would take under similar circumstances, with someone else being harmed as a consequence.[1] In a business setting, the measure of a "reasonable person" is probably a professional of similar experience as the business owner being sued, the idea being that the business owner hasn't done something, or not done something, that would be expected of a generic professional in that line of work. For a freelancer who wants to reduce risks, this means being a smart and informed professional by staying aware of your field's evolving best practices, and implementing them wherever possible.

Negligence has a broad scope. Much of the time, doing something negligent might not get you sued, but it will probably be embarrassing and damaging to your business. A copyeditor who accidentally deletes a citation from a scholarly article could expose her client to charges of plagiarism. A wedding photographer who mishandles a memory card and loses pictures of a ceremony will be lucky to escape with just forfeiting his fees for the shoot. The digital age has given rise to new sources of negligence. Misdirected e-mails, insecure cloud storage, and loose behavior on social media are just a few ways a freelancer can wind up in trouble.

---

[1] Nolo. 2016. *Nolo's Free Dictionary of Law Terms and Legal Definitions.* s.v. "negligence." www.nolo.com/dictionary, (accessed December 9, 2016).

Jim the Deadbeat

Jim has earned a substantial sum of money from a contract that pays in installments, only he hasn't been doing the work he promised to do. As he has been paid, he's immediately transferred the funds from the company to himself as salary, and used them to pay off student loan debt. When the client discovers that Jim hasn't been performing, it sues and wins. When it learns that Jim has taken the money it is owed, it argues that it should be able to reach past the Jim's company to recover directly from his personal assets. In this example, Jim has acted badly, by knowingly accepting payment for services he wasn't performing, so the fairness scales tip in the client's favor.

Paula and the Prying Husband

Paula is a successful fiction editor who works from a home office for major publishing firms on high-profile novels. She has formed a limited liability company, Superstar Editorial LLC, to house her business and enter into contracts with publishers. Among the contracts are strict nondisclosure agreements, which threaten significant damages against Superstar Editorial LLC if it should breach its obligations. Paula keeps her client's files on her computer, which does not require a password to access.

One afternoon, Paula tells her husband about an exciting new novel she is working on. The novel is by a famous author the husband enjoys. Later that evening while Paula is out at a freelancer association meeting, her husband accesses her computer and e-mails a copy of the new novel to himself and to his buddy, who also loves the author's work. After too many glasses of wine the buddy posts a copy of the file to Facebook, where it is downloaded hundreds of times before he realizes his mistake. The publisher quickly discovers the leak and identifies Paula as the probable source. It successfully sues Superstar Editorial LLC to recover, among other things, $2 million in lost revenue that the publisher estimates the leak will cause. Paula figures she'll have to put her business into bankruptcy, but at first she's not worried about her personal assets. That is, until in the damages phase of the trial the publisher puts forward the argument that Paula's LLC should be disregarded, and it should be allowed to recover its $2 million award from Paula personally.

From Paula's perspective, there are lots of bad facts in this story. The two big mistakes Paula made were telling her husband about her project, which violated her nondisclosure obligations, and then not securing her client's files, which the publisher will argue was negligent in light of the files' substantial commercial value.

In the litigation, the publisher's lawyers dug into Superstar Editorial LLC by asking for its minute books, bank records, and other evidence of its separateness from Paula's personal life. Among other bad facts, they discovered that Paula had been cutting corners, using her company's bank account to pay for her child's daycare services and her monthly mortgage payments. In a business where the company's assets can be reduced to a computer and a bank account, it's starting to look like Paula is facing serious financial consequences.

The point of these above examples is to emphasize that just having a legal entity is not enough to protect yourself against personal loss. It is important to take other defensive steps, like protecting client files, respecting contractual obligations, and taking seriously your legal entity's formalities. If you can afford it, buying professional liability insurance that includes coverage for litigation costs is another good way to limit risk, in part by offering litigators an alternative deep pocket to your own, one that will be defended by seasoned attorneys.

CHAPTER 6

Naming Your Business

Every freelancer needs to decide what to call their business. Sole proprietors often just do business in their own name. Doing so simplifies the business licensing process, can avoid a few minor administrative hassles, and can avoid trademark pitfalls that come with coined terms and clever turns of phrase. Of course, many freelancers, even those who work as sole proprietorships, will want to explore more creative names for their businesses. For those who will be forming legal entities, the choice of name involves additional considerations, because the company's name needs to be available at the state level before it can be used.

This chapter's focus is on the legal technicalities of choosing a name, rather than branding considerations. Branding is a complex, nuanced subject. Regardless of the legal form your business will take, choosing a name that represents who you are and what you do is an essential part of marketing yourself to clients. Your company's name will be all over the place: on your business cards, on your website, on social media. It should resonate and communicate. Take the time to explore the branding advice available on the web. If you have the resources, consider hiring a branding professional to help you sort through your ideas. Talk to your friends and colleagues about your name ideas to get their impressions, and ask them for suggestions. Brainstorm and keep lists. Chances are good that the first few names you pick won't work, for reasons you won't recognize until you've researched them further.

State Requirements

There are relatively few restrictions on how a legal entity is named. States often will reject names that are offensive (profanity or racial slurs, although a recent Supreme Court case suggests that such limits may be an unconstitutional restriction of free speech[1]) or misleading (for example, most states don't allow companies to use the words "bank" or "trust" unless they are going to be in those industries). Knowing your state's restrictions can be helpful, so you know what to avoid, but it's unlikely that the handful of restricted words will matter to most freelancers.

A requirement that knocks out many business names is **availability**. To use a name, it can't already be taken by someone else in the jurisdiction where the company is registering, whether that's at the local level for licensing, or at the state level when forming a new entity. Just how close a name can be to an existing name varies from place to place, and can even depend on the person reviewing it. Most jurisdictions will ignore details like punctuation (ABC, LLC blocks ABC LLC), articles (Superstar Editorial LLC blocks The Superstar Editorial LLC), or different versions of statutory suffixes (ABC Inc. vs. ABC Corp.). Most jurisdictions provide online databases of existing names to help you determine if your preferred name is already taken.

Most jurisdictions provide online databases of existing names to help you determine if your preferred name is already taken. Online databases don't always include names someone else has **reserved** for future use, so there's always a chance that your name will be rejected due to one of these "hidden" registrations. To avoid this problem you may need to call or, in some places, submit a written request. Such formal name clearances generally cost $20 to $50.

The Many Pitfalls of Trademark Law

If you plan to use your company's name to promote your business, you'll need to consider whether it threatens to conflict with any existing

---

[1] In *Matal v. Tam*, 582 U.S. ___ (2017), an all-Chinese rock group called The Slants successfully sued for the right to register the band's name as a federal trademark. The Supreme Court upheld a lower court's ruling that struck down a provision of U.S. trademark law prohibiting registration of trademarks that "disparage . . . persons, living or dead . . . or bring them into contempt, or disrepute." Lanham Act, 15 USC § 1052(a) (2017). Among other things, the disparagement clause had been used to prevent racially offensive terms from being registered as trademarks. The court unambiguously stated that the First Amendment protects even offensive speech, raising serious doubts about the validity of state restrictions on offensive terms in business names.

trademarks. Adopting a name that is already subject to another person's trademark rights can force you to change your company's name, derailing your branding efforts and costing money and time as you hunt down a new name, get new business cards printed, change e-mail addresses, and build a new website. Better to put in the work beforehand to make sure your name doesn't cause more trouble than its worth.

By itself, a business's legal name, as shown on its state registration documents or business licensing documents, isn't a trademark until it meets the use standard described below. One way to think about the distinction is that a business's name is a noun, while a trademark is an adjective. A trademark *describes* something about the goods or services that carry it.

In simple terms, a trademark is a word, phrase, or symbol that is **used in commerce** to identify the source of goods or services. The law imposes a pretty low bar on what constitutes "use in commerce" for purposes of establishing trademark rights. Putting a name on promotional materials that get handed out to potential clients is one way a name goes from being just a legal formality to being used as a trademark. In the right circumstances, using the name on a website can also meet the use in commerce standard.

State and federal laws prevent someone from adopting a trademark that is **confusingly similar** to a trademark that is already in use or that someone has claimed for use in the future. Whether two marks are confusingly similar is determined by a complex and varied set of legal standards that, in simple terms, look at whether a hypothetical consumer is likely to confuse the two marks when encountering them in the marketplace. The analysis used to determine the likelihood of confusion considers a range of factors, including the similarity of the marks, the similarity of the goods or services, and the relative strength of the senior mark.[2]

Ordinarily, owners can only enforce trademark rights in connection with the specific products or services where their trademarks are in use.

---

[2] *Polaroid Corp. v. Polarad Elecs. Corp.*, 287 F.2d 492 (2d Cir. 1961). Nolo Press provides a good introduction to the likelihood of confusion standards. Richard Stim. "Likelihood of Confusion: How Do You Determine If a Trademark is Infringing?" http://www.nolo.com/legal-encyclopedia/likelihood-confusion-how-do-you -determine-trademark-infringing.html, (accessed August 2, 2017).

There are nearly four dozen categories, or **classes**, of products and services, and the scope of a registration tends to be limited to the specific products or services that use the mark. If Superstar Editorial LLC is an appealing name for your editing business, but your searches turn up businesses in unrelated industries (for example, Superstar Plumbing, Superstar Laundry, and Big Superstar Family Buffet) it might not be a problem, because the other uses of "superstar" have no overlap with your planned line of work. On the other hand, if your search uncovers a registration for Superstar Publishing that specifies editorial services or even something to do with publishing in its description, there may be too much overlap.

Simply knowing the goods and services in the registration of an existing trademark isn't enough to confirm that it doesn't pose an infringement risk. The relative **strength** of the marks needs to be weighed.[3] In part this is done by placing the marks within a **spectrum of distinctiveness**.[4] This approach looks at the character of the trademark itself, placing it into one of five categories. The categories, from weakest to strongest are as follows:

1. **Generic** terms can't be registered as trademarks, at least in connection with a product they normally refer to. No one can register the term "apple" for apples. A trademark can also become generic through routine use. Aspirin is just one example of a trademark that became a generic term.[5]

2. **Descriptive** marks use terms that are directly related to the goods or services involved. For example, "crunchy" for apples. To be registerable, a descriptive mark needs to first establish **distinctiveness** through its use.

3. **Suggestive** marks might say something about the goods or services, but they require some mental effort to draw the connection. "Microsoft" is a common example of a suggestive mark.

---

[3]For examples and further explanation of the strength of trademarks, see Daniel A. Tysver, "Strength of Trademarks," BitLaw.com (2015), http://www.bitlaw.com/trademark/degrees.html, (accessed August 2, 2017).

[4]The spectrum of distinctiveness began with *Abercrombie & Fitch Co. v. Hunting World*, 537 F.2d 4 (2nd Cir. 1976).

[5]*Bayer Co. v. United Drug Co.*, 272 F. 505, 512 (S.D.N.Y. 1921).

4. **Arbitrary** marks generally are common terms used in an otherwise nonsensical context. Think of "Apple" for computers, or "Adobe" for software.

5. **Fanciful** marks have no meaning other than as a trademark. They are treated as inherently distinctive, meaning they are relatively easy to register and they enjoy the greatest protection from infringement.

The spectrum of distinctiveness can be a helpful way to think about your own business name. Inventing a name that fits within the strong end of the spectrum—something arbitrary or fanciful—can be a way to increase the chances that your name will be available at the state level and not infringe on an existing trademark. On the other hand, if you invent a term and find that someone else is already using it, be careful. The owner of a fanciful trademark holds a lot of cards.

Famous trademarks are given an extra layer of protection against infringement that crosses the usual boundaries between classes. McDonald's Corporation has a tight grip on terms beginning with "Mc," making it a risky bet to name your photography business "McPhoto." Likewise, the camera manufacturer Nikon probably would object to a business calling itself "Nikon Copyediting." One reason to avoid famous trademarks is that they tend to be guarded by a team of dedicated trademark attorneys. Famousness is a frustratingly fuzzy topic, because you might have no awareness of a name that meets the legal standards of "fame." That's why it's important to look carefully at all potential conflicts.

Personal Names as Trademarks

A personal name is considered descriptive for trademark purposes, meaning that although most surnames aren't registerable as trademarks, they can become protectable by acquiring distinctiveness. In 1997 basketball legend Kareem Abdul-Jabbar sued a professional football player named Karim Abdul-Jabbar for trademark infringement, on the grounds that the football player's adopted name would be commercially damaging to the hall of famer's brand. Even if you choose to do business under your own name, some vetting is still a good idea.

Trademark can be a tricky area to navigate, in part because existing trademarks aren't necessarily easy to identify. A name's use of the $^\circledR$ symbol (reserved for registered marks) or the ^{TM} superscript is an immediate indication that the owner of the name claims trademark rights. But if you encounter a name that doesn't have one of these symbols, there are steps you can take to evaluate its status. The U.S. Patent and Trademark Office (PTO) hosts a searchable database (TESS) of all the trademarks that have been registered under federal law.[6] States also have trademark registries of their own, and many people who plan to only do business in one state might opt to register with their state instead of going through the expense of a federal registration. But searching these databases isn't enough, because a trademark owner has rights even if the trademark isn't registered. So-called common law trademarks that exist outside of the registration system can still be used to force you to change your business's name.

How much time and money you want to spend on sorting through all this will depend on your appetite for risk. Businesses that will invest heavily in promoting their names as a brand probably should invest the thousands of dollars that's usually necessary to get professional trademark help. If your branding goals are more modest, the cost of professional trademark advice may be harder to justify. You can go a certain distance by doing your own searches, using Google and searching databases at the PTO and state trademark registries. The trouble is that amateur searches aren't likely to capture the full universe of potential conflicts. And when your search results come back it can be hard to know if your name really conflicts with a potential match without getting some professional advice.

One partial solution is to hire a **trademark screening service** to conduct professional searches of your favorite name. These services use sophisticated methods to find potential conflicts that can be difficult to find without specialized skills. They will provide you with a ream of search results, and many of them offer additional analysis for a fee.

The most reliable approach is to hire a **trademark lawyer** to help you parse the results of your searches. Unless you plan to register your

---

[6]U.S. Patent and Trademark Office, Trademark Electronic Search System, accessible at http://tmsearch.uspto.gov/.

trademark, a lawyer's analysis needn't be a hugely expensive process. Still, you must decide for yourself if the risks justify the additional cost.

Should You Register Your Business Name as a Trademark?

Registering your business name or logo as a trademark offers several benefits. It allows you to add the ® symbol to your mark, putting other potential users on notice that you have a claim over your business name. It provides nation-wide protection of your brand, which is useful if you plan to expand your business beyond your home region. It gives you extra leverage to defend your name against potential infringers. And it can help you if you have to sue to protect your name. The downside, of course, is that registration costs money, primarily due to legal fees associated with preparing the paperwork and maintaining the registration. If you do plan to register your business name as a trademark, you may want to explore filing an intent-to-use registration, which allows you claim rights over a name while you invest in its initial promotion. Anyone who plans to register a mark should work with a lawyer at the naming stage to avoid costly false starts.

One Way to Approach the Name Vetting Process

There are lots of great branding resources on the Internet to help new business owners get started on their naming journey. Once you have a list of favorite names, they'll each need to be evaluated for potential conflicts and risks. Here is one way to approach vetting your list.

1. **Impromptu searches.** Once you have a list of possibilities, it's time to search for them using an online search engine. The goal at this point is to weed out names that are already being used enough to have a web presence. Casual searches aren't enough to reach a reliable conclusion that a name is free for use, but they can quickly identify clear conflicts. Searches can also turn up unexpected problems with a name. To avoid offending potential clients you may not want to choose a name that has an obscene meaning if translated into Spanish, for example.

2. **Technical searches.** As the list of potential names dwindles, you'll want to start searching specific places for conflicts:

   a. *State database.* Keep in mind that search tools can lack the sort of fuzziness that makes Google so useful, so you might need to come at the search in a few different ways. Starting with a key term might be a good starting point (searching "Superstar" instead of "Superstar Editorial"). Also, be sure to confirm that your state's website includes name reservations. If it doesn't, you may need to call. Many states also offer name preclearances for a fee, though it isn't usually required.

   b. *Local database.* Your chosen name needs to be available in the county (and city, if it has separate business licensing rules from your county) where you will be doing business; if you work in more than one county, you'll need licenses in each. Sole proprietorships that adopt names other than their owners' must file a fictitious business name statement as part of the business licensing process. These filings don't appear on state websites, but will prevent you from getting a business license unless you first adopt a DBA (short for "doing business as") name that doesn't conflict. A DBA adds costs and hassle, as your DBA needs to show up everywhere the company's formal name appears. Better to adopt a name that you know works at every level.

3. **Check into domain names.** If you plan to have a website for your business, now is a good time to visit a domain name registrar's site to see what domains are available that suit your name. Unless your name is something wildly unique, chances are that the most desirable domain name is already taken. Sorry, Superstar Editorial LLC, but "superstar.com" is probably long gone. Instead, play around with variations that you think will work. Although a domain name's availability might not be a good reason to keep or toss a potential name, having a straightforward domain name can be a valuable marketing tool. A domain like suprstaredtrl.com isn't easy to remember or spell, but superstareditorial.com might work. If you have your heart set on a specific URL, you might have to pay someone to let you have it.

4. **Conduct a trademark analysis of your favorite names.** Once a name makes it through all the other types of searches, it's time to

conduct a search of the PTO database (accessible at http://tmsearch
.uspto.gov/) to see if anyone has claimed a trademark that's similar to
your preferred name. Search using a few different variations of your
name and take advantage of the system's truncation tools. Chances
are good that you'll see quite a few matches or near matches. You'll
need to dig into each of the matches to see if they are in a related
line of work to your own. If after conducting this process you're
not feeling reasonably sure about whether your name is safe from a
trademark standpoint, consider hiring a screening service to conduct
a professional search and analysis of your preferred name. And if
you think the cost is justified, ask a trademark lawyer to look at the
search results.

CHAPTER 7

Taxes

Tax considerations are a critical part of organizing a business. The cost of operating a business, from setup fees to legal expenses, can ultimately be dwarfed by the effect that taxes have on how much money a freelancer gets to pocket. This chapter introduces some basic concepts about business taxation. Tax is a large and byzantine topic, one that is mostly beyond the scope of this book. The goal of this chapter is to touch upon some basic topics that might factor into your decision about how to structure your business, so you can do further research on areas of particular relevance to your situation. Readers should note that as this book was going to press Congress was debating significant changes to the way business income is taxed. The values and examples in this chapter can help you come to grips with important tax concepts, but many of the specifics may be changing soon.

Obtaining a Federal Tax ID Number

Every small business should have its own IRS **employer identification number**, or EIN. The IRS offers a fast, free online system for obtaining an EIN,[1] or you can fill out Form SS-4 and submit it by fax or mail. The EIN is unique to your business and helps the IRS link up your business's taxable events to the business and ultimately to you as the owner.

One good reason to get an EIN is to avoid having to disclose your Social Security number to clients. Chances are that every business client will ask for an IRS Form W-9, on which you can provide your Social Security number or, alternatively, your EIN. Businesses that pay contractors $600 or more in a year are required to report the payments on

---

[1] Internal Revenue Service. 2017. Apply for an Employer Identification Number (EIN) Online. www.irs.gov/businesses/small-businesses-self-employed /apply-for-an-employer-identification-number-ein-online.

Form 1099-MISC, which includes the contractor's tax ID. You'll receive a copy of the 1099 from the client and will report it as part of your annual tax return.

State Franchise Taxes

States usually impose taxes other than income tax on business entities. An important one to know about is **franchise taxes**, which can be a flat fee or can vary depending on the company's income. Franchise taxes can be an ugly surprise, in part because they aren't subject to the sort of deductions that are available in the income tax world. For example, California imposes a minimum franchise tax fee of $800 on all LLCs and corporations doing business in the state.[2] Texas does not impose franchise taxes on businesses with less than $1,100,000 in annualized revenue, but businesses below the threshold must file a No Tax Due Report with a total revenue figure and other details.[3] Know your state's requirements before you decide what kind of entity to form.

Employment Taxes

Freelancers who are used to working for an employer may be surprised to learn just how expensive employment taxes can be. In federal terms, "employment tax" means a combination of two taxes on wages: Social Security (in 2017, 6.2 percent paid by both the employee and the employer, for a total of 12.4 percent of wages) and Medicare (in 2017, 1.45 percent paid by both the employee and the employer, for a total of 2.9 percent of wages); these two taxes combine for a 15.3 percent tax rate on wages in 2017.[4] In 2017, the maximum wages subject to Social Security tax is $127,200; there is no equivalent cap for the Medicare tax.[5]

---

[2] For more information see the State of California Franchise Tax Board website, www.ftb.ca.gov.

[3] For more information see the Texas Comptroller of Public Accounts website, comptroller.texas.gov.

[4] Internal Revenue Service. 2016. *(Circular E), Employer's Tax Guide*, Publication 15, Cat. No. 10000W. pp. 23-24. Note that an additional Medicare tax of 0.9 percent is collected on wages in excess of $200,000 in a calendar year. *Id.*

[5] *Id.* p. 23.

Your state may collect other kinds of employment tax as well. Ordinarily, both the employer and employee pay the tax on the salary paid to the employee, but only the employer gets to claim employment taxes as a deductible expense. In a self-employed situation, you will still be able to deduct half of your employment taxes, but the math can be more or less favorable depending on how your company pays you and how your company is treated for tax purposes. A bit later we'll look at an example of how this could play out.

Income Tax Treatment of Business Entities

For federal income tax purposes, one can think of the business structures discussed in this book as falling into two categories: pass-through or tax-regarded. Each of these categories is defined by how tax authorities treat the business and its distributions to its owner.

Category 1: Pass-through Entities

In a pass-through business structure, the owner (or owners) of the business report the company's income and losses on their personal income tax returns on IRS Schedule C. The business entity is **disregarded** for federal income tax purposes. Sole proprietorships, which have no formal existence apart from their owner, fall into this category. Partnerships and LLCs also receive this treatment by default, though they can elect to be treated as a tax-regarded entity (see below) by filing the appropriate election with the IRS and, quite often, state tax authorities. Conversely, a corporation must choose to be treated as a pass-through entity, otherwise it will have to pay separate income taxes.

Keep in mind that an entity being pass-through doesn't free it from filling out paperwork; every business entity, even pass-through entities, files forms with the IRS at tax time. This ensures that the IRS knows what to look for on the owners' personal returns. Federally disregarded entities can also be subject to other kinds of tax that don't get passed through to their owners, such as employment, state, and local

taxes. For example, California collects a 1.5 percent income tax from
S corporations.[6]

Category 2: Tax-Regarded Entities

A tax-regarded business entity files its own tax return and pays income
taxes on any money it earns, applying corporate income tax rates. By
default, a corporation is treated as a separate taxpayer from its shareholder.
An LLC can elect to be treated as a corporation by filing an election with
the IRS. Any earnings the owner receives from the company are taxed
again at personal tax rates. This is often described as **double taxation**,
because both the company and its owner are paying income tax.

To reiterate, here's a quick summary of how these categories break
down for the most likely business forms for freelancers:

Pass-through Entities	Tax-Regarded Entities
Limited Liability Companies (by default)	Limited Liability Companies (by election)
S Corporations (by election)	C Corporations (by default)
Sole Proprietorships	

The Potential Benefits of Tax-Regarded Entities

At first blush double taxation sounds bad. The government takes a cut
of whatever revenue the company earns, and takes another cut of what
the freelancer takes from the company as earnings. Nonetheless, operating a tax-regarded company can be preferable in certain tax situations,
especially in businesses with high income. There are several basic reasons
for this.

**First, a tax-regarded entity can claim a tax deduction for salary
paid to its owner-employee.** The IRS permits entities taxed as corporations to deduct salary only if the salary is not "excessive." To determine

---

[6] State of California Franchise Tax Board. 2016 California Tax Rates and Exemptions.
2017.www.ftb.ca.gov/forms/2016-California-Tax-Rates-and-Exemptions.shtml?WT
.mc_id=Business_Popular_TaxRates#ctr.

whether the salary is excessive, the IRS will look at a number of factors, including typical salaries of comparable professionals. Any salary paid in excess of this amount will be treated as **dividends**. Unfortunately, the IRS doesn't have strict guidelines on what qualifies as "excessive" salary, so if you expect to be a high income earner, it is worth consulting with a tax adviser to figure out what makes sense for your situation.

Second, dividends are not subject to employment taxes. Although dividends are not deductible expenses for a tax-regarded entity, they are also not subjected to employment taxes. Using the dividend approach, the company must pay its employee-owner a "reasonable" salary, essentially according to the same vague rules used to identify "excessive" pay. Then the company, following the requirements of the company's organizing documents and state law, declares a dividend, distributing its surplus to the shareholder as a return on the shareholder's investment in the company. The owner pays ordinary income tax on the resulting payment, but avoids the employment tax hit.

Dividends are subject to a number of technical requirements that must be followed to avoid the IRS treating them as taxable salary. First, they need to be formally approved by a written consent of the company's management, that is, by a corporation's director or by an LLC's member. Skipping this step and simply transferring money from your company's account to your personal account will look like ordinary salary; going back to paper over these transfers can be considered fraud. Second, dividends normally can only be declared if the distribution to the owner will not cause the company to become insolvent, that is, the company's debts won't exceed its assets after the dividend is paid. This can be trickier to determine than it might seem. Because of these technicalities, freelancers who want to take advantage of the dividend approach quite often need the help of a tax professional, accountant, or lawyer to make sure everything is done the right way.

A third potential advantage of tax-regarded entities is that they can retain profits for operating expenses. A tax-regarded entity need not pass on its cash to its owner. Instead, it can hold on to its cash and use it for future expenses, like buying expensive equipment. This avoids double taxation altogether by not converting the money into salary or dividends, and avoids employment taxes.

High income earners (roughly speaking, those who earn $100,000 or more annually) would probably benefit the most from having a tax-regarded entity. By taking a portion of profits as salary, and the rest as dividends, the result may be a lower tax bill. There are some expenses associated with doing things this way, such as the need for a formal payroll system, and the increased necessity of professional help, that might make it undesirable for a lower income earner.

A Tax Example: Tanisha

Here is a simplified example that shows how operating a tax-regarded company might benefit its owner. This example leaves out a lot of important factors that contribute to a calculation of income tax, like standard deductions. The point is to help you understand how "double taxation" might be a net benefit.

Tanisha is a freelance videographer with a corporation, Super Video Inc. Over the course of a year, the company has $100,000 in earnings. The company had $10,000 in unreimbursed expenses for things like phone, Internet, travel, equipment, and professional fees. The example uses the tax rates applicable to a single filer in 2017.

Tanisha may have good reasons for leaving Super Video Inc. as a *tax-regarded entity*, thanks to the advantages she gains from the relatively low corporate tax rate, the deductibility of wages, and the limited applicability of employment taxes. She pays herself a salary of $50,000, which she determines is about the average for videographers in her area. She plans to use $10,000 of the company's remaining after-tax profits to upgrade her cameras and lenses, so she leaves that portion in the company's account and plans to transfer the company's after-tax surplus to herself as a dividend. Using these figures, the company has a total of $63,825 in deductible expenses ($50,000 in salary, $3,825 in employment tax [7.65 percent of $50,000], and $10,000 in ordinary expenses). This leaves the company with $36,175 in taxable income. The company's income will be taxed at the corporate tax rate (15 percent in 2017 for federal taxes), leading to a corporate federal income tax bill of $5,426.

After factoring out $10,000 to be retained by the company for future equipment purchases, Tanisha puts on her director hat to sign a short written consent authorizing the company to pay her a shareholder's dividend of $20,749, representing the remaining surplus profits for the year. On her personal tax return, Tanisha pays the other, nondeductible half of the employment taxes on her $50,000 salary (again, $3,825, or 7.65 percent of $50,000) and personal income taxes on the $50,000 salary plus $20,749 in dividends. Tanisha's tax rate tops out at 25 percent, which results in a personal income tax of $13,425.[7] Tanisha's bottom line for the year is a net personal income of $53,497, with $10,000 retained by the company, and a combined tax bill of $26,502.

If, on the other hand, Tanisha has properly filed a Subchapter S election to have the IRS treat Super Video Inc. as a pass-through entity, the tax treatment is quite different. Because Super Video Inc. is an S corporation, it does not pay dividends. As a technical matter, S corporations pay *distributions* to their shareholders, who must report their allocation of the company's net profits and losses on their personal income tax returns regardless of whether they actually receive payments from the company. This means that Tanisha reports *all* of the company's earnings and losses on her personal tax return, so it will not save her any money to retain cash at the company. As a starting point, she has earned $90,000, or the company's net receipts ($100,000) less its ordinary expenses ($10,000). She must pay both her personal half and the company's half of the employment taxes due on this amount (15.3 percent of $90,000, or $13,770). She gets to deduct the business's half of this amount, $6,885, from her $90,000 income for calculating her personal income taxes, netting her an adjusted gross income of $83,115. Her personal income tax on this amount is $16,517, leaving her with a net personal income of $59,712 and a total tax liability of $30,287.

---

[7] The example uses 2017 single filer tax rates for personal income. Income taxes are calculated progressively. In 2017, the progressive tax brackets were 10 percent for the portion of income that is from $0 to $9,325, 15 percent for $9,326 to $37,950, and 25 percent for $37,951 to $91,900. Kyle Pomerleau. 2016. "2017 Tax Brackets." https://taxfoundation.org/2017-tax-brackets/, (accessed August 1, 2017). In 2017 the corporate income tax rate was 15 percent on taxable income up to $50,000. See PwC. 2017. "United States Corporate – Taxes on corporate income." http://taxsummaries. pwc.com/ID/United-States-Corporate-Taxes-on-corporate-income, (accessed August 1, 2017).

Is your head hurting yet? Here's a summary to help you sort out the numbers:

Tax-Regarded Entity (C Corporation)

Receipts:	$100,000
Non-Salary Expenses (Deductible):	−10,000
Salary Expenses (Deductible):	−50,000
Employment Tax Expense (7.65%) (Deductible):	−3,825
Pre-Tax Income:	**36,175**
Corporate Income Tax (15%):	−5,426
After-Tax Retained Income:	**30,749**
Retained for Use by Company:	10,000
Dividend to Freelancer/Shareholder:	−20,749
Freelancer Wage Income:	$50,000
Freelancer Dividend Income:	20,749
Freelancer Gross Income:	**70,749**
Freelancer Employment Tax (7.65% of wages):	−3,825
Freelancer Income Tax:	−13,425
Freelancer Net Income:	**53,497**
Combined Tax Liability:	**$26,502**
Combined Post-Tax Retained Profits:	**$63,497**

Pass-through Tax Entity (S Corporation)

Receipts:	$100,000
Non-Salary Expenses (Deductible):	−10,000
Pre-Tax Income:	**90,000**
Employment Tax (15.3%; 50% deductible)	−$13,770
Freelancer Personal Income Tax:	−16,517
Freelancer Net Income:	**59,712**
Combined Tax Liability:	**$30,287**
Combined Post-Tax Retained Profits:	**$59,712**

In this example, Tanisha saves more than $3,700 in taxes by operating as a tax-regarded entity, thanks to three things. First, the corporate tax rate is lower than the personal rate. Second, by having the company retain some earnings instead of paying them out as wages, she has avoided paying employment or personal income tax on that amount. And third, Tanisha avoids paying employment taxes on a significant chunk of her profits by taking it as a dividend rather than salary.

Keep in mind that the example above is simplified almost to the point of being unrealistic. Importantly, it doesn't take into account state income and employment taxes, which can have a big effect on a business's bottom line. There are also important long-term tax consequences that can come into play, especially for businesses that will have substantial assets like expensive video equipment. When it comes to shut down the company, the tax consequences of liquidating the company's assets can be significant.

There are two key points to this example. First, it shows that the choices you make about how your business is organized and run can have a big effect on your financial outcome. Second, it shows the value of running through a few tax scenarios using your anticipated revenue and expenses. Explore how state and federal tax rules treat your big expenses, like health care premiums and equipment. Would you benefit from keeping cash in your business, where it will be taxed at lower rates than your salary? Do you anticipate earning enough to take advantage of a mixed strategy of salary and dividends? Consider using one of the many online tax calculator tools to help you in your research. You may be pleasantly surprised by how much you can save by making certain choices.

The Mechanics of Tax Treatment Elections

As discussed in Chapter 4, corporations that operate with their default treatment as tax-regarded entities are called C corporations, or C corps. Corporations can elect to be treated as pass-through entities, by becoming S corporations, or S corps. LLCs are the opposite of corporations: by default, an LLC is a pass-through entity, but it can elect to be taxed as a C corporation.

Freelancers who form a legal entity and plan to use the default tax treatment, there are no special steps to take at the time the company is formed, other than obtaining a tax ID number for the business. But for those who plan to change the company's default treatment, there are important steps that must be taken on time to avoid a lot of costly headaches.

Corporations that wish to be treated as S corporations file **IRS Form 2553 Election by a Small Business Corporation**, also known as a **Subchapter S election.**[8] This form gets signed by each of the corporation's shareholders. As of this writing, **the form must be filed with the IRS no more than 2 months and 15 days after the beginning of the tax year when the election is to take effect**. The IRS treats the 2-month period as ending on the day before the corresponding day of the first month. Keep in mind that the first tax year for a new corporation is always shorter than a full year, because the company will be formed after the January 1 holiday. For example, a corporation that is formed on May 23 measures its 2 months to July 22, then adds 15 days to arrive at a deadline of August 6.

A member of an LLC that wishes the IRS to treat the company as a corporation—that is, as a C corp—can file an **IRS Form 8832 Entity Classification Election.**[9] The form needs to be filed with the IRS within 75 days of its effective date. New businesses probably will want the effective date to be their formation date.

Missing the deadline for a Subchapter S or Form 8832 election ordinarily means that the election won't be effective until the next tax year. A company that files late ordinarily gets taxed according to its default rules for the year in which the late filing was made. The IRS allows companies that accidentally miss the deadline to argue that it should be treated as though the filing was made on time, by asserting that they missed the

---

[8] Internal Revenue Service. 2017. "Form 2553, Election by a Small Business Corporation." www.irs.gov/uac/form-2553-election-by-a-small-business-corporation, (accessed August 1, 2017).

[9] Internal Revenue Service. 2016. "Form 8832, Entity Classification Election." www.irs.gov/uac/form-8832-entity-classification-election, (accessed August 1, 2017).

deadline for "reasonable cause" and have taken diligent steps to correct the mistake. The IRS doesn't have an official explanation of what "reasonable cause" means, but authorities suggest that it is fairly forgiving of situations where the responsible person simply forgot to take care of the filing.[10] Nonetheless, being at the mercy of a petition to the IRS is not a good place to be. Better to complete your election filing on time.

James and the Giant Mistake

James is an experienced freelance medical editor who works for several large pharmaceutical firms. For various reasons, he and his accountant decide that his best option is to form an S corporation for his editing business. The accountant handles the paperwork for forming the company, using standard forms. When the company is formed, the accountant forgets to file the company's Subchapter S election.

Two years ago, James, relying on his accountant's word, has filed his taxes with the assumption that the corporation's election to be treated as an S corporation is effective. As his business changes, James decides that the corporation is no longer needed, so he files the paperwork to dissolve it, again using his accountant's advice to complete the transaction.

After the company is dissolved, James gets a letter from the IRS notifying him that his corporation has failed to pay taxes and is now subject to penalties. James promptly finds a new accountant and also decides to hire a tax lawyer to help him navigate the mess. Fixing the problem will not only require paying penalties and professional fees, James will have to revive his dissolved corporation, revise his tax filings of the last 2 years, and submit a new Subchapter S election together with an explanation about his accountant's negligence in hopes that he can still get the tax treatment he wanted for a company that he thought was already wound up.

---

[10] Internal Revenue Service. 2017. "Late Election Relief." www.irs.gov/businesses/small-businesses-self-employed/late-election-relief, (accessed August 1, 2017).

CHAPTER 8

Contracts

Entering into contracts is one of the most important roles of a legal entity. When your company enters into a contract with another person or business, you put your counterpart on notice that the company, and not you personally, owns the obligations of the agreement. This is an important way for freelancers to manage the day-to-day risks of doing business, and is also an important way of maintaining the distinction between your business entity and yourself as the owner. This chapter offers a few steps a freelancer can take to ensure that business contracts are properly drafted.

At the most abstract level, a contract is an enforceable **bargain** between or among two or more people (including corporate "persons") in which one or more person has made a **promise** to do or not to do something in exchange for **consideration**, and the parties have **manifested their mutual assent**.[1] Consideration might be something with concrete value, like money, or something intangible, like an agreement to perform in-kind services.[2] A contract needn't be a formal document with ink signatures. It can be inferred from a collection of e-mails or, least desirably, simply a verbal agreement, provided that the key terms of the bargain between the parties can be determined. Among other things, this means that it is easy to form an enforceable contract that doesn't binds your legal entity or include all the terms you'd like. There are some easy steps you can take to avoid these pitfalls.

---

[1]Restatement (Second) of Contracts §§ 1, 2, 17 (Am. Law. Inst. 1932).
[2]*Id.* at § 79.

Binding a Legal Entity

Contracts are a key part of the corporate separateness idea that we looked at in Chapter 2. Once formed, the legal entity should "own" the business. That means, among other things, making sure that it is specifically named in any agreement relating to the business.

Formal Agreements

A formal, written contract can come in many different styles. It might be a preprinted form with blanks for the freelancer's name, or it might be a Word document that a client asks you to mark up with the details of your business. In such cases, the important thing to remember is that the contract should be entered into using the business entity's full legal name, not your own. A typical contract calls for names in two places: in the contract's **preamble**, usually the first paragraph that describes the parties, and on the **signature page**. Also look out for sections in the middle of the contract that ask for your company's notice address and other details.

Example Preamble

This Independent Contractor Services Agreement (this "Agreement") is made between Big Spender Client Corporation, a Delaware corporation ("Client") and **ABC Freelancer LLC, a California limited liability company** ("Contractor"), effective as of _____, 2017.

On the signature page, the freelancer signs the contract on behalf of the LLC. The title the freelancer uses is determined in the company's organizing documents. In this example, from the same contract as our example preamble, the owner of ABC Freelancer LLC has named herself the company's president:

Example Signature Block

CONTRACTOR:
ABC Freelancer LLC
By:
Name: M. Freelancer
Title: President

Notice that the freelancer's personal name doesn't appear except as an officer of the company. An incorrect formulation might have appeared in the preamble, putting just M. Freelancer's name in the blank before the parenthetical with "Contractor" in it. It might also have appeared on the signature page, putting M. Freelancer's name where the company's name appears.

"Informal" Agreements

A contract can form without anyone signing a paper document. In the 47 states that have adopted the Uniform Electronic Transactions Act, an e-mail or other electronic format (such as a voice recording) can create a perfectly enforceable contract.[3] Even an oral conversation can be enough to form a contract. Here the freelancer needs to be especially careful, because it can be easy to speak in personal terms ("I'll do this for you.") that can lead to personal liability unless the client knows that it is ultimately dealing with the legal entity, and not with the freelancer. It is always a good idea to negotiate the terms of a project and then summarize all of the terms in a proposal for the client to accept. Even if language implying personal obligation has been used to that point, asking

---

[3]Every state other than Illinois, New York, and Washington has adopted a version of the Uniform Electronic Transactions Act. National Conference of Commissioners on Uniform State Laws. 1999. *Uniform Electronic Transactions Act.* www.uniformlaws. org.

the client to approve a final summary that puts the obligations squarely on the business entity can be enough to ensure that the business entity's limited liability sticks.

Example Simple E-mail Proposal

Dear Client,

Thank you for engaging ABC Freelancer LLC to copyedit the manuscript of your novel, *The Dullest Book Ever*. Based on my review of the 50,000 word version you sent to me on April 5, we have agreed to a flat fee of $1,000 for one detailed pass through the draft. My review will be completed by May 15. Payment in full will be due within 30 days of delivery of the fully edited manuscript.

Sincerely,

M. Freelancer, President

ABC Freelancer LLC

When using this strategy, keep in mind that contracts can't arise without both sides indicating agreement. It is not enough to send an e-mail like the example above; the client needs to acknowledge its acceptance of your terms. As my law school contracts professor liked to say, **silence is not acceptance**.

Contracts with Clients

In an ideal world, no freelance job should be started without having an agreement in writing setting out the obligations of both sides. This is true of small jobs as well as large ones.

Finding Work through Freelancing Websites

Freelance job sites such as UpWork.com or Freelancer.com typically dictate the terms that apply to jobs arranged through them. In these cases, a separate contract isn't necessary, because the job market sites have already provided one. In fact, having a separate agreement usually violates the terms of use of such sites and can get you banned from using them. If you get work through these sites and plan to form a legal entity, be sure to find out if the sites you use will let you bind your legal entity. If you can't put your legal entity on the hook your work will be as a sole proprietor. It is important to remember that revenue you generate outside of the umbrella of your legal entity gets treated separately from your company's revenue for tax purposes.

The specific form a contract takes is not important so long as it reflects the terms of the deal and shows agreement by both sides. A contract need not be on paper with real signatures; an e-mail exchange setting out the parameters of the job can suffice. A common freelance practice is to prepare a proposal, either in an e-mail or in a more formal document, and ask the client to approve it. When taking this route, it's a good practice to not start work before the client has specifically indicated agreement with the terms you've provided. The last thing you want to do is spend 20 hours on a project only to have the client suddenly take issue with your fee structure.

Having a form of agreement on hand is a good idea. The specific kinds of issues that a contract should cover will vary by industry and can be influenced by state law. Generally speaking, a contract should reflect all the terms of the deal that you've discussed with the client, as well as any protective provisions you feel are appropriate for the job. Here are a few things that a contract should cover:

- The specific scope of the services you will provide.
- Pricing and payment terms, including how long the client will have to pay after receiving the invoice and how you handle late payments.
- All important deadlines and provision for how deadlines get changed, such as acceptable notice periods.
- Provision for termination, which might include a "kill fee" owed to you for work you have already completed.

Some freelancers may want to include other language in their standard contracts. A photographer might ask for permission to include images from a client's shoot on the photographer's website. Many photographers also specifically retain copyright in the photos they shoot. An editor might want to emphasize that the client bears ultimate responsibility for the work.

Clients may ask for specific terms, too. They may even have a form of agreement that they use with independent contractors. Don't sign or agree to any contract without reading it. If there are terms you don't understand, ask the client to explain them. Be especially aware if the client's form agreement imposes special obligations upon you, such as:

- Confidentiality obligations (a.k.a. nondisclosure agreements).
- Restrictions against trading the client's stock, if the client is a public company. Pay special attention to the scope of these clauses, because they can apply to your close family members as well.
- Assignments of intellectual property rights in the work, especially if you are not willing to make such assignments without extra compensation.
- Restrictions against working for a client's competitors, sometimes referred to as noncompetition clauses.

Always make sure you know the exact scope of your obligations under these kinds of restrictions. For example, if a noncompetition clause doesn't specify exactly who you can't do business with, it is essential to demand clearer language that provides you with the necessary information so you can comply. Also, restrictions like these often come with their own timeframes, usually lasting a while after your work for the client is finished. If you intend to agree, for example, to keep your work for the client confidential, you need to take that obligation seriously and keep track of when it expires. It is a good idea to put final deadlines on your calendar.

Negotiation is almost always an option. If a client offers a form contract with terms that you find unacceptable, it rarely hurts to push back. Marking up the contract to strike out the specific language you don't like is the best way to approach this. The worst that can happen is the client rejects your changes. In some cases, very small business clients may refuse to negotiate because they don't want to pay their lawyer to review your changes. Some clients, like many government agencies, are prohibited from deviating from their standard contracts. If the client won't budge, then you will have to decide if agreeing to the contract is worth the risk.

Contracts with the Owner

Many freelancers will have business-related contracts that are the freelancer's personal obligation. Cell phone services and home Internet connections typically straddle work and personal lives. Even if the freelancer is treating these sorts of agreements as 100 percent business expenses, the obligation to pay their bills will rest with the freelancer personally unless the business assumes them or, more likely, enters into a separate contract of its own. Ordinarily it isn't necessary to go that far, and for a small freelance business it usually isn't practical anyway.

The freelancer may still prefer to be reimbursed for expenses related to these personal contracts, by having the business pay them. Depending on how the legal entity is structured, the freelancer can get into trouble doing this the wrong way. Just having the company pay the bill can create two problems. First, it intermingles personal and business assets by using company funds to pay a personal obligation. Second, if the company is tax-regarded it can create taxable income for the freelancer, because the company is essentially assuming the freelancer's debt.

These are steps you can take to avoid these problems:

- Pay personal obligations with personal funds (your own credit card or checking account, not the company's).
- Routinely document expenses by gathering together copies of bills and evidence that they were paid. Keep these "expense reports" well organized.
- Once the expenses are properly documented, the company can reimburse the freelancer from the company's account.

CHAPTER 9

Putting It All Together

Whew! We've covered a lot of complicated topics, with plenty of details to sort through. Now is a good time to take a step back and look at the big picture. Remember, the goal of this book is to give you a foundation for making informed decisions about how to structure your business. There are a lot of ways to go about this. The best way is to talk to professional advisers—a business lawyer, a tax expert, and perhaps an accountant—who can answer your questions and, most importantly, raise issues that you haven't thought about. Because a freelancing business probably isn't a particularly complicated organization, it shouldn't cost a fortune to get sound, basic advice. Nonetheless, you can save time and prepare to make better choices by organizing your thought process.

Here are some steps to help you consolidate what you've learned from reading this book for answering the two big questions: should I form a legal entity for my business, and if so, what kind? At this point it's worthwhile to put aside some of the book's topics that aren't germane to these central questions. Choosing a name for your business is fun, but it can wait. Also, it's worth stepping away from all the technical details the book has thrown at you about how LLCs and corporations are run. If the answers to the really big questions point toward a certain business form, it will be worth the effort to master the little administrative details, no matter how obscure they seem now.

Step 1: Evaluate Your Business Risk

The decision about whether to form a legal entity for your business could be couched in another way: why shouldn't I operate as a sole proprietorship? As we covered in Chapter 1, the main reason for forming an LLC or corporation is to manage your personal risk. When it comes to business entities, risk management is primarily about two things: taxes and legal liability. Understanding your risk, and your appetite for risk, is a vital part of the decision you face.

Think about the kinds of risk you face in your business. Do you work with litigious clients? Do you work on high value, sensitive materials? Do you travel a lot for your business? Think about how your business will develop in the future. If your goals will take you into riskier territory than you've explored so far, then that should factor into your choices. Putting your company on the hook is much easier if it is already organized when you start a big, risky project.

Think about your tolerance for risk. Do you have property that you want to shield from potential business creditors, like a home or retirement account? How willing are you to expose your personal assets to the risks you expect to face?

Step 2: What Business Form Best Manages Your Risk?

We looked at the three main forms a freelance business can take: sole proprietorships, LLCs, and corporations. Because the state where you live can have such a big influence on which of these forms is best for you, this book probably can't give a definitive answer about which one of these is best for your situation. But if we put aside the small stuff, like how these entities get formed and managed, we can get a big picture sense of them. Use the information in Table 9.1 to compare the key characteristics of the different business types.

Of course, this table is only a starting point. You may have other ideas, especially after doing your own research about your state's rules. It might help you to put together a table like this with your own categories and concerns. After pulling together your table, chances are you'll have a pretty good idea of which direction you want to go.

Step 3: Think about Your Existing Business

If you have been operating as a sole proprietor for a while, chances are that your business has accumulated some assets (hard assets like a computer, and soft assets like client testimonials) and has some administrative

Table 9.1 Legal entity comparison

	Sole proprietorship	Limited liability company	Corporation
Liability of the owner	Unlimited personal liability.	Limited to the amount contributed to the company. Might be less robust than a corporation in some states.	Limited to the amount contributed to the company. Traditionally the strongest legal liability protection.
Costs to organize	None.	$100 to $200 depending on state fees, plus any professional fees.	$100 to $300 depending on state fees, plus any professional fees.
Costs to manage	Negligible. • Local business licensing. • Fictitious business name statement filing if operating under an assumed name.	Modest. • Local business licensing. • State franchise taxes. • Annual statutory reporting (~$20 to $200).	Modest. • Annual business licensing renewals. • State franchise taxes. • Annual statutory reporting (~$20 to $200). • In some situations might require a bit more professional guidance to maintain good governance.
Federal income taxes	Income and loss are reported on owner's personal income tax return (IRS Schedule C). All profits are subject to self-employment tax.	By default, income and loss pass through to its member's personal income tax return (IRS Schedule C). All profits are subject to self-employment tax. An LLC can elect to be taxed as a corporation.	By default, treated as a separate taxpayer from its shareholder. Its net profits are subject to corporate income tax rates. The shareholder pays personal income tax on wages and other income from the corporation. Entities taxed as corporations can take certain deductions that are not available to pass through entities, such as paid salary, certain insurance premiums, and certain taxes. Savings on employment taxes might be achieved by treating some payments to the shareholder as dividends rather than salary. A corporation can elect to be taxed as a sole proprietorship by filing an subchapter S election and becoming an S corp.
Administrative burden	No special requirements.	Minimal. • No special recurring meeting requirements. • Easy annual reporting. • Good contract practices are important.	Can be a bit more burdensome. • May have annual meeting requirements, satisfied by preparing short written documents. • Annual reporting may require some additional paperwork. • Good contract practices are important. • Those using dividends as a tax strategy must properly document the payments.

details (accounting records, websites, service contracts). For a lot of free-lancers, their biggest business assets will be their personal brand and their stable of existing clients. How will you address your approach to rebrand-ing under a new legal entity, so your existing and potential clients know that the professional behind your sole proprietorship will be operating under a new name? Do you have long-term contracts that you'll want to move into a new entity? If you do, what do they say about transferability?

Also think about how you currently manage your business, and how that might need to change if you form a legal entity. Are there steps you'll have to take to get organized, like finding a new bank for business pur-poses that could take you some time? Will you need a new website or e-mail address?

Step 4: Map Out Costs and Consider Taxes

Before settling on a business form, it's worth doing a rough analysis of your expected income and expenses. On the income side, think about how much you expect to make each year. Then, make a list of your antici-pated routine business expenses. This can start with your state's fees for forming a legal entity and keeping it in compliance. Typically, this infor-mation is readily available on a state's Secretary of State website. Will you be buying health insurance coverage through your company? How about liability insurance? What kinds of service contracts and other business expenses do you anticipate your company having?

Once you have an estimate of income and expenses, consider first if your expected income makes you comfortable with the costs of owning a company. Then, think about if you might benefit from your company being a tax-regarded entity. If a big expense is tax deductible for a C cor-poration, but not deductible for an S corporation, it could turn out that having your company pay separate taxes is actually an advantage. If you're struggling to figure these things out, track down a tax expert and run your situation by them. Making good choices at the start can save you a ton of money in taxes over the long run, so a professional's fees will be money well spent.

After going through these steps, hopefully you'll know more than enough to make the right choice for your business. The good news is that once you've made a choice and gotten organized, the tedious work of setting up your company will be behind you. You can turn to the fun of running your business with the confidence that your risks are under control and your bottom line isn't smaller than it ought to be.

Further Reading and Resources

One reason this book exists is that finding clear, concise information about organizing a freelance business is like drinking from a fire hose. If you'd like to track down more specific information to suit your situation, there are good resources available. Freelancer organizations like the Editorial Freelancers Association can be a great resource for printed materials as well as advice from peers. My starting point for reliable, plain language guides on legal topics is Nolo (www.nolo.com). Nolo puts out dozens of books covering all manner of business law topics. The best resources will be tailored to your state's requirements. You can also probably use the vocabulary from this book to find advice on specific topics posted online from lawyers in your state, though you'll have to sort through a lot of potentially confusing information that isn't relevant to you.

If you plan to keep costs down by trying to organize your business yourself, without involving a lawyer, it is important that you find a reputable and reliable source for template documents, especially an LLC's membership agreement or a corporation's bylaws. These documents can be pretty simple in a single-owner situation, but it's critical that they not only meet your state's current requirements, but also don't add unnecessary complexity to your company's governance requirements. Also, remember that forms available on the Internet aren't always updated as laws change. You can save yourself a lot of money and headache now by paying a little for someone to help you put together the right paperwork.

CHAPTER 10

Businesses with More Than One Owner

As freelancing evolves, more and more people who identify themselves as freelancers are thinking about joining forces to do business together, either informally through closed networks, or as formal co-owners of a legal entity. Running a business with other people has plenty of advantages. Partners can divide the expenses and administrative work associated with running the business, and leverage their distinct talents to build a stronger brand. Businesses with more than one owner are also inherently more complicated than solo businesses, enough that it is beyond the scope of this book to address all of the important issues that business partners need to address when organizing their business. This chapter briefly introduces the business entity forms that are commonly used by businesses with multiple owners, including extra considerations for LLCs and corporations. We'll also review some of the core ideas that business partners need to resolve when organizing a legal entity.

Two Points about Business Partnerships

Before we dig into the legal entities themselves, let's think about a couple of topics that don't come up for solo business owners: looking after your own interests in a partnership context, and the obligations joint owners owe to one-another.

Protecting Yourself

When going into business with others, it is vitally important to protect your own interests. No one else will do that for you, and that includes the lawyer the business hires to draft the company's paperwork. When a business hires a lawyer, the lawyer is required to treat the business itself, not its owners, as the client. Although the owners have plenty of say about how the business is organized, the lawyer can't separately advise each owner about how their rights might be affected by the decisions made in connection with organizing the company. A good business lawyer will advise the owners to seek their own, independent counsel on the potential legal, financial, and tax implications of forming a business.

A big reason for taking steps to protect yourself is the risk that the business won't succeed, or worse, your partner will turn out to be unethical or downright criminal. In a very small business, chances are good that everyone involved will have some degree of authority over the company's assets, including bank accounts. It is important that the company's organizing materials address problems like insolvency before getting started.

Think of the company's organizing documents like a prenuptial agreement. The business partners might love each other at the beginning, but if things go badly, or one of the partners runs off with the company's pot of gold, the company's legal framework will provide an important tool for managing not just business risk, but your personal risk as a partner of the business.

Obligations to Your Partners and the Business

When people go into business together they have obligations to one-another and to the business entity itself. The law calls these obligations **fiduciary duties**. They chiefly arise when someone has management responsibility over a business: for example, the members of a member-managed LLC or the directors of a corporation. This probably captures everyone involved in most small freelance partnerships. Breached fiduciary obligations tend to be a prominent part of litigation between former business partners, so it is worth knowing what your obligations are.

There are two major fiduciary duties: the duty of loyalty and the duty of care. The **duty of loyalty** requires the business manager to be honest while dealing with the company. The manager must put the company before her own self-interest, and must avoid conflicts of interest that could undermine the manager's ability to make good choices for the company.

The expectation is that the manager will direct new business opportunities to the company instead of taking them for herself. The **duty of care** requires managers to act responsibly and in good faith, taking reasonable steps to ensure that the company is well run. This doesn't mean that the manager has an obligation to make the company *succeed*. The **business judgment rule** provides that bad decisions that cause a business loss aren't by themselves a breach of a manager's duty of care so long as the manager makes the decisions in good faith. A manager might run afoul of the duty of care by being sloppy or careless in operating the company, for example by signing up for expensive services that the company can't afford and doesn't need.

The specific obligations of a corporate shareholder or director, LLC member, or corporate officer vary somewhat by the state where the company is organized. They can also often be changed in a company's organizing documents. For example, owners who have other business interests will probably want to document specific limits to their duty of loyalty to the partnership so they can continue to operate their side businesses without breaching their fiduciary obligations. This is an area where it can be especially useful to have an independent lawyer looking out for your interests.

Bear in mind that fiduciary duties are *personal* obligations. Breaching them gives the other owners of a business a cause of action to sue in court for damages. The owner who breaches a fiduciary duty might be forced to use personal assets to repay financial losses. This is an important risk to consider when thinking about going into business with someone else.

General Partnerships: The Default Rule

When two or more individuals take steps to form a business together but they haven't yet organized a legal entity, they are deemed to be in a **general partnership**. Like a sole proprietorship, the partners in a general partnership bear personal liability for the obligations of the company. Any profits of the partnership are divided between the partners however they deem fit, and reported on the partners' personal income tax returns. In a general partnership, each partner has **equal power to bind the general partnership** to obligations, or to dissolve it. Likewise, the partners are **jointly and severally liable** for the business's debts, meaning that creditors can go after any of them to recover what is owed, regardless of who was responsible for the original debt. Then it's up to the partner who got stiffed to go after the other partners to balance things out. If one partner has more assets than the others, that partner could end up with the most to lose.

Here's an example of how a general partnership can fall to pieces. Freelancers A, B, and C agree to form a graphics design business. A and B are fresh out of college and have no assets other than their exceptional design skills. C, on the other hand, owns a house and has a nice investment portfolio. Although they plan to eventually organize the business in a more formal way, they let such things slip. B signs a contract for a big project that pays a refundable advance of $25,000 in anticipation that the business will need to hire a few subcontractors to make the deadline. Unfortunately, A has decided that working isn't much fun, so he takes the $25,000 and catches a plane to Costa Rica to live for a while on the beach. Thrown into chaos, the business can't deliver on the big contract, and the client demands the return of the $25,000. When B and C fail to pay up, the company sues, going after only C, the one with the assets. In a situation like this, C might have no choice but to sue A, since he's stolen from B and C. But he might also need to sue B, who is just as responsible for the company's debts as C, even though both of them are victims of their partner's theft.

If A, B, and C had formed a limited liability entity, the story might have been different. Although the client still would sue the business, it would need additional facts to overcome the company's limited liability protections to reach B and C personally (see Chapter 5 on how this works). The business, in turn, would have reason to go after A. But if A was gone, and the company had nothing to pay back to the client, the company, at worst, might be driven into bankruptcy. C would not be at risk of losing his house, and wouldn't need to sue his friend B as part of the fallout.

Although there are risks to operating as a general partnership, there are several advantages that might make it an attractive alternative for new businesses. Like the sole proprietorship, a general partnership has no special formalities for its formation, so its initial administrative costs are low. A simple agreement covering the basics of the business's operation can suffice while the business's assets and risks are small. Such an agreement usually covers financial questions, such as how much each partner will contribute to the company and what happens if a partner doesn't want to contribute more in the future. It might also discuss ownership of the intangible assets of the business (for example, the company's name, logos and other trademarks, and any copyrighted works the partners might create, like website content or software code). The partners might also agree to milestones that will trigger the formation of a more formal business entity.

LLCs and Corporations

It probably comes at no surprise that LLCs and corporations are both popular choices for businesses that will be owned by more than one person. A good reason for this is that the owners don't need to reinvent the wheel to get their company organized. Unless the owners want to do something unusual, the company's attorney can probably prepare the governing documents without a huge extra investment over what a single owner would require. All of the principles discussed in Chapters 3 and 4 still apply to a company owned by multiple people, but there are a few extra questions that the owners will need to address at the outset. Here are a few examples:

- **Management obligations and rights.** Who will manage the company's financial records? Who will take responsibility for the company's statutory obligations, like business licenses and annual reports? Will all of the owners have formal management responsibilities (serving as corporate directors, or as an LLC's managing members) or will some owners prefer to defer those responsibilities to working through questions like these at the beginning will avoid headaches later.
- **Capital obligations.** Document how a company's owners contribute capital to the company, and their obligations to contribute more if the company needs it. Depending on state rules, contributing more money to the business might be doable without issuing more stock. It is important to properly document

owner contributions to avoid misunderstandings, in part because **member and shareholder contributions of capital aren't debt.** Co-owners should recognize that the company doesn't owe them interest on the money they contribute and has no obligation to pay anything back. Owners stand to lose their entire investment if the company goes broke.

- **How will the owners get paid?** The company might pay the owners a salary, or it might declare distributions as the company gets paid by clients. What happens if the company is going through a dry spell? How much should the company retain in its account to pay its bills? These kinds of questions tend to get complicated and many small businesses work with accountants to help sort through them.

- **Voting rights.** Decide how the owners will make decisions about the company, especially about how it is managed. Allocating voting rights based on capital contributions is one way to do this, but it isn't the only way. For example, an LLC's operating agreement can provide that each member will have an equal say in the management of the company, regardless of how much money each member contributes to the business.

- **Restrictions on sale.** Most small business owners do not want their partners to be able to freely sell their interest in the company. The owners might conclude that they do not want to allow any kind of sale, or they might allow for rights of first offer or rights of first refusal, which give the nonselling partners a chance to buy out the selling owner.

- **Disaster planning.** The owners should agree about what happens if things go badly for the business (for example, bankruptcy), or something happens to a partner (death or incapacity). Owners of small businesses will often agree that the other owners have a right of first refusal to buy the share of the company owned by someone who dies or retires. How the company's assets get distributed if it is wound up also needs to be covered. This is a broad category that needs the guidance of a lawyer to cover everything. Statutes that govern business entities will have a lot of default provisions covering many of these issues, but a company's organizers are often free to depart from the default rules if desired.

Limited Partnerships

The **limited partnership** was the first limited liability entity that offered pass-through tax treatment for its ownership. In a sense, the LLC is a refinement of the concept of the limited partnership. Quite often, their management and maintenance obligations are quite light, determined almost entirely by the documents the partners prepare when the partnership is organized.

Limited partnerships are formed by filing a **declaration of partnership** (or sometimes a certificate of limited partnership) with the state. The partners enter into a contract called a **limited partnership agreement**, which sets out how the company will be managed. These documents can be remarkably simple for a simple business structure, though the limited partnership agreement can get more complicated if the partners want to organize their management or financial obligations in a way that departs from the statutory defaults.

Limited partnerships have two types of partner: limited and general. Like corporate shareholders, **limited partners** do not take part in the management of the company. In turn, they do not have personal liability for the debts and obligations of the company. The **general partner**, on the other hand, manages the company and *does* bear liability for its obligations. A general partner usually cannot be a limited partner, and in some jurisdictions such an arrangement can cause the partnership to immediately dissolve, essentially reducing it to a general partnership. The general partner acts as the limited partnership's agent and handles all of the company's day-to-day operations, from running bank accounts to signing contracts.

A general partner can be a natural person, or it can be a legal entity. Sophisticated businesses that use limited partnerships as part of their tax structuring strategy will often form special purpose entities, such as an LLC, to serve as the general partner and shield "upstream" owners from liability for the partnership. Technically, an individual freelancer could form a single-member LLC to serve as general partner in a limited partnership, with the freelancer holding the limited partner interest. Although there is nothing stopping a freelancer from doing this, it is unlikely to offer any advantages over just using an LLC or corporation for the business.

Glossary of Select Terms

agent for service of process. The person formally designated by a business entity to receive notices from the state and service of lawsuits. All states require that the agent of service of process be a state resident, and usually require the agent to have a street address (no P.O. boxes). The business owner may serve as agent for service of process, or a service provider can be hired to avoid disclosing the owner's home address. If you plan to name someone other than yourself as agent for service of process, it is vitally important that he or she know about and agree to the arrangement, and that they know to notify you if their address changes. Some states require agents for service of process to submit a separate, signed consent to the appointment.

articles of incorporation (also: certificate of incorporation). Formal, legal document filed with the state's Secretary of State to cause a corporation to be formed.

capitalization. Refers to how a company's owner has paid for his or her share of the company's ownership. In many states, paying real value for ownership rights (as represented by a LLC's **membership interests** or a corporation's **shares**) is an important part of properly organizing a legal entity and preserving **limited liability** protections.

C corporation (also: C corp). The name used to describe a corporation that is treated as a separate taxpayer from its owner for federal income tax purposes. Corporations are automatically C corporations when they are formed; they must file special paperwork with the IRS and state tax authorities to be treated differently (see: S corporation). The name comes from the section of the tax code covering such entities (Subchapter C).

certificate of organization (also: articles of organization, certificate of formation). Legal document filed with a state's Secretary of State to cause a LLC to be formed.

close corporation. A special form of corporation that allows the corporate shareholder to directly manage the company. Not available in all states.

company. A generic term that can refer to any type of business, however it is organized.

contract. An enforceable bargain between or among two or more people (including corporate "persons") in which one or more person has made a promise to do or not to do something in exchange for consideration, and the parties have manifested their mutual assent.

corporation. A legal entity formed by filing appropriate paperwork with a state's Secretary of State office. A corporation's key characteristics are: (1) limited liability of its owners (see: shareholder), (2) management by a board of directors, and (3) separate tax treatment by default (see: C corporation) with an option to be treated as a pass-through entity (see: S corporation).

creditor. A creditor is anyone who is owed money. Ordinarily, a business's creditors will fall into two categories: (1) lenders and (2) service providers that the business owes money to. A creditor can also be someone who has successfully sued the business and has received a court judgment for a cash award. Creditors who are not paid on time can seek to recover what they are owed through legal means (lawsuits) or by using the mechanisms available to them through contract (for example, they might put a lien on real estate or a car that is owned by the business or its owner).

director. An individual elected by a corporation's shareholder(s) to manage the day-to-day affairs of the company. A corporation's sole shareholder can also be its sole director.

double taxation. A situation where a business entity pays separate income taxes from its owner, who also pays income taxes on any distributions from the business. Although double taxation can result in lower net earnings, in some situations double taxation can be an advantage.

fiduciary duty. An obligation a company's directors, managers, and/or officers owe to the company and its ownership. Fiduciary duties include the duty of loyalty and the duty of care.

fictitious business name statement. A document that is typically required to be filed with business license applications for businesses that will use a name other than the owner's personal name.

franchise taxes. Special annual taxes imposed by many states on legal entities. Franchise taxes can be thought of as the price the state puts on the privilege of doing business in the state.

freelancer. An individual professional who works for clients on a contract, project-by-project basis.

general partnership. The default form for a business owned and operated by two or more people (each a general partner) who have not organized a separate legal entity. A general partnership's key characteristics are: (1) comes into existence as soon as its owners begin to do business, (2) joint and several personal liability of its owners, and (3) each general partner has equal authority to bind the company.

governance. Generally refers to the management of the business organization itself. Includes the company's organizing documents, the records of its owners and managers, and the steps required to maintain the company in good standing with the state where it is organized.

incorporator. The individual who signs and submits a corporation's articles of incorporation to the state. The incorporator bears personal responsibility for the corporation until the corporation's shareholder and board of directors are put in place.

indemnification. A promise by a company to assume any personal obligations of the company's officers or directors that arise in connection with their work for the company. Such obligations can include legal fees associated with defending against litigation, but can also include smaller things like administrative fees and other expenses. For example, an officer who gets a parking ticket for failing to feed a parking meter because she is in a meeting with a big potential client can ask the company to cover the cost of the parking ticket. But take care: administrative fees like parking tickets aren't tax deductible as a business expense,[1] though attorney fees and other costs related to fighting a ticket probably are. For a freelance business, unless state law requires the company to indemnify its officers or directors, chances are that it isn't necessary or desirable to have an indemnification clause in the company's formation documents. It usually only comes up if outsiders will be serving in a management role.

limited liability. A limited liability business entity shields its owners from personal liability for the debts and obligations of the company. The scope of limited liability is discussed in Chapter 5.

limited liability company. A legal entity formed by filing appropriate paperwork with a state's secretary of state office. A limited liability company's key characteristics are: (1) limited liability of its owners (see: member), (2) ability of its owners to directly manage the affairs of the business, and (3) pass-through tax treatment by default, with an option to elect to be taxed separately.

limited partnership. A legal entity formed by filing appropriate paperwork with a state's Secretary of State office. A limited partnership's key characteristics are: (1) limited liability of its limited partners, who do not have direct management authority over the company and (2) unlimited liability of its general partner, who manages the business on behalf of the limited partners.

member. The owner of a limited liability company.

membership interests. The unit of ownership in a limited liability company. Can be expressed in whole values (e.g., 10 units) or as a percentage (e.g., a 100% membership interest). A limited liability company's organizing documents determine how membership interests are issued, valued, and documented.

merger clause. Language in a contract providing that the contract contains the complete agreement between the parties, regardless of promises made outside the contract. A helpful way to avoid confusion about the full scope of a deal.

operating agreement (also: **limited liability company agreement**). The primary governing document of a limited liability company. Sets out the rights and duties of the company's member, determines how the company will be managed, and specifies various mechanics of the company's governance.

officer. Any individual who is appointed by a company's governing body to carry out specific duties. Any kind of business can appoint officers. A freelancer might want to take the title of President of his or her business, though more creative titles can be used if desired.

pass-through tax treatment. An entity that federal and state tax law treats as a pass-through vehicle does not pay separate income taxes from its owner. Instead, the owner reports the profits and losses of the company on the owner's personal income tax returns. Keep in mind that pass-through treatment is only related to income tax, and may not apply to other kinds of tax, like franchise taxes. Pass-through entities are sometimes referred to as being disregarded for tax purposes.

---

[1] "No deduction shall be allowed . . . for any fine or similar penalty paid to a government for the violation of any law." INTERNAL REVENUE CODE, 26 U.S.C. § 162(f) (2017).

par value. A minimum cash value of each share of the company's stock, typically a trivial value, such as a tenth of a penny ($0.001) per share or even less. Some states require a corporation to assign a par value to its shares. It is specified in the company's articles of incorporation. If the company has specified a par value, a shareholder must pay at least that amount for shares to be considered properly issued. Modern corporate statutes have done away with the antique notion of par value, but if your state requires it, it is important to make sure that the par value is built into the amount you pay for the company's shares.

personal liability. In the context of business entities, personal liability means that the owner of a business is directly responsible for all of the obligations of the business, from fees owed to service providers to debts owed to creditors. Where personal liability applies, the owner's assets (home, car, savings) are at risk of being taken to pay debts to creditors. Sole proprietorships and general partnerships are the two most common types of business entity that impose personal liability on their owners.

preamble. A contract's opening paragraph. Usually includes the contract's date and the names of the parties.

S corporation, or S corp. A corporation that has elected to be treated as a partnership or pass-through entity for federal tax purposes, by filing the appropriate paperwork (see: Subchapter S election) with the IRS. State tax authorities may require a similar election to have federal treatment applied at the state level.

securities. A representation of a *passive* ownership interest in a company, such as stock of a corporation. State and federal laws tightly regulate the offer and sale of securities.

shareholder (also: stockholder). An owner of shares of stock of a corporation. To become a corporate shareholder, one typically needs to pay value for the shares, and the company's formal records must reflect the ownership. A corporation that doesn't follow the formalities necessary to complete the issuance of shares to a shareholder can lose its limited liability protections.

stock. A corporation's units of ownership. Also referred to as shares. A corporation's stock is a form of security that is subject to securities laws.

sole proprietorship. A business owned by one person and not organized as another, more formal business entity type. A sole proprietorship does not exist apart from its owner, who bears personal, unlimited liability for the business's obligations.

subchapter S election. A form submitted to the IRS that causes a corporation to be taxed like a partnership (or sole proprietorship) for federal income tax purposes (see: S corporation).

trademark. A word, phrase, drawing, or combination of these that is used in commerce to indicate the source of the good or service.

written consent. A document that formally memorializes an approval of actions to be taken by the company. For a limited liability company, written consents are signed by the company's member. For corporations, written consents might be signed by the shareholder (for example, to appoint a director) or by the company's board of directors. Written consents take the place of holding meetings, and are a common governance strategy for small businesses.

Index

OTHER TITLES IN OUR BUSINESS LAW COLLECTION

John Wood, Econautics Sustainability Institute, *Editor*

- *Preventing Litigation: An Early Warning System to Get Big Value out of Big Data* by Nelson E. Brestoff and William H. Inmon
- *Understanding Consumer Bankruptcy: A Guide for Businesses, Managers, and Creditors* by Scott B. Kuperberg
- *The History of Economic Thought: A Concise Treatise for Business, Law, and Public Policy, Volume I: From the Ancients Through Keynes* by Robert Ashford and Stefan Padfield
- *The History of Economic Thought: A Concise Treatise for Business, Law, and Public* Policy, Volume II: After Keynes, Through the Great Recession and Beyond by Robert Ashford and Stefan Padfield
- *Buyer Beware: The Hidden Cost of Labor in an International Merger and Acquisition* by Elvira Medici and Linda J. Spievack
- *European Employment Law: A Brief Guide to the Essential Elements* by Claire-Michelle Smyth
- *When Business Kills: The Emerging Crime of Corporate Manslaughter* by Sarah Field and Lucy Jones

Business Expert Press has over 30 collection in business subjects such as finance, marketing strategy, sustainability, public relations, economics, accounting, corporate communications, and many others. For more information about all our collections, please visit www.businessexpertpress.com/collections.

Business Expert Press is actively seeking collection editors as well as authors. For more information about becoming an BEP author or collection editor, please visit http://www. businessexpertpress.com/author

Announcing the Business Expert Press Digital Library

Concise e-books business students need for classroom and research

This book can also be purchased in an e-book collection by your library as

- a one-time purchase,
- that is owned forever,
- allows for simultaneous readers,
- has no restrictions on printing, and
- can be downloaded as PDFs from within the library community.

Our digital library collections are a great solution to beat the rising cost of textbooks. E-books can be loaded into their course management systems or onto students' e-book readers. The **Business Expert Press** digital libraries are very affordable, with no obligation to buy in future years. For more information, please visit **www.businessexpertpress.com/librarians**. To set up a trial in the United States, please email **sales@businessexpertpress.com**.

www.ingramcontent.com/pod-product-compliance
Lightning Source LLC
Chambersburg PA
CBHW062034200326
41519CB00017B/5032